Citizen Perspectives on Community Policing

SUNY SERIES IN NEW DIRECTIONS IN
CRIME AND JUSTICE STUDIES
AUSTIN T. TURK, EDITOR

CITIZEN PERSPECTIVES ON COMMUNITY POLICING

A Case Study in Athens, Georgia

BRIAN N. WILLIAMS

STATE UNIVERSITY OF NEW YORK PRESS

Published by
State University of New York Press, Albany

© 1998 State University of New York

For information, address State University of New York
Press, State University Plaza, Albany, N.Y. 12246

Production by E. Moore
Marketing by Fran Keneston

Library of Congress Cataloging-in-Publication Data

Williams, Brian N., 1967–
    Citizen perspectives on community policing : a case study in
Athens, Georgia / Brian N. Williams.
        p.   cm. — (SUNY series in new directions in crime and justice
studies)
    Includes bibliographical references and index.
    ISBN 0-7914-3703-5 (alk. paper). — ISBN 0-7914-3704-3 (pbk. :
alk. paper)
        1. Police—Georgia—Athens—Public opinion. 2. Police—Georgia-
-Athens—Attitudes. 3. Community policing—Georgia—Athens—Public
opinion. 4. Public relations—Police—Georgia—Athens. 5. Urban
poor—Georgia—Athens—Attidudes. 6. Athens (Ga.)—Public opinion.
I. Title. II. Series.
HV8148.A69W55 1998
363.2'09758'18—dc21   97-17203
                                                                CIP

10 9 8 7 6 5 4 3 2 1

To those who toiled and strove for the success of others. To the memory of Lula Chandler; Morris Williams, Sr.; James Napoleon Greene, Sr.; John Frank Green; Johnnie Mae Green; Eva O'Neal Armstrong; Paul Williams; Dennis Hadley; Richard Hadley; and a host of other relatives and friends who reinforced the morals and ethics instilled by my parents and my community. You may be gone, but not forgotten.

CONTENTS

TABLES AND FIGURES

PREFACE

The assessment of citizen satisfaction with local governmental services and the delivery and distribution of these services plays an essential role in evaluating, restructuring, and implementing effective governmental policies. This assessment is particularly important in inner-city areas where residents have expressed pronounced concerns with the delivery of police services. Citizen evaluations, then, provide public officials with important cues about public perceptions of the performance of local agencies (Skogan, 1979). This particular study examines the opinions held by inner-city residents in Athens, Georgia, on community policing as well as the coproduction of law enforcement.

A qualitative, nonexperimental research design using focus-group interviewing was used to collect information about the perceptions of East Athens residents and selected officers in the Athens-Clarke County Police Department. Nine citizen focus groups and one officer focus group were assembled. Additionally, two one-on-one interviews were used in the data-collection process. The related group discussions and interviews within this study occurred in 1994.

In general, the research revealed citizen dissatisfaction with police service delivery and skepticism toward community policing in particular; little evidence was found to the contrary. The pattern of dissatisfaction was consistent among the majority of focus groups. This fact is particularly noteworthy, considering the volunteer respondents were active, positive residents in the community. The results of this research contain important information for community policing endeavors in other locales and will aid future attempts to coproduce public services in poor, minority communities.

The findings from this study highlight several important policy implications for the design, expectation(s), implementation, and evaluation of community policing efforts. Specifically, this research suggests that: police departments must commit to the organizational philosophy and strategy of community policing; extensive departmentwide "start-up" training is a prerequisite for community policing success and must be adhered to; community preparation is a necessity for community involvement and community policing success; community residents must be targeted and recruited as community policing officers; police departments must disseminate realistic time projections for community policing to temper residents' expectations; research on the evaluation of community policing and other efforts to coproduce public services must be expanded to include qualitative as well as quantitative methods.

These findings highlight the need for citizen assessment in the formulation, implementation, and evaluation stages of governmental programs and policies that have community involvement and assistance at their core.

ACKNOWLEDGMENTS

First and foremost, I would like to thank my Heavenly Father, my Lord and Savior Jesus Christ, and the Holy Spirit for leading, guiding, comforting, and providing for me throughout the long and tedious journey from research to publication. During this process, I learned that faith is the cornerstone for success, nothing is too hard for God, and how truly dependent I am upon Him for all things.

> Abide in me, and I in you. As the branch cannot bear fruit of itself, except it abide in the vine; no more can ye, except ye abide in me. . . . If ye abide in me, and my words abide in you, ye shall ask what ye will, and it shall be done unto you. (John 15:4–7)

> My grace is sufficient for thee: for my strength is made perfect in weakness. Most gladly therefore will I rather glory in my infirmities that the power of Christ may rest upon me . . . for when I am weak, then am I strong (2 Corinthians 12:9–10).

> They that wait upon the Lord shall renew their strength; they shall mount up with wings as eagles; they shall run, and not be weary; and they shall walk, and not faint. (Isaiah 40:31)

Have not I commanded thee? Be strong and of a good courage; be not afraid, neither be thou dismayed: for the Lord thy God is with thee whithersoever thou goest. (Joshua 1:9)

Special appreciation is expressed to my loving family and in-laws. My wife Carla; my daughter Carmen; my mother Frances; my father Morris; my grandmother Princetta; my father-in-law Barner; my late mother-in-law Johnnie Mae; my brothers Morris, Roddrick, Richard, and Robert; my sister Stephanie; my sister-in-law Tangela; my brother-in-law Antione; and a host of other relatives, neighbors, and friends who have offered prayers, words of encouragement, and generous support. Also, a special thank you to my grandmother Mary—the memories of her prayers and faith shall live with me forever.

Sincere gratitude goes to Susette M. Talarico for her continuous guidance and words of encouragement. I would also like to thank Jerome S. Legge, Jr.; Hal G. Rainey; Arnold Fleischmann; and Pamela Kleiber, members of my doctoral committee, for generously sharing of expertise, critical reading of this study, and advice.

I am indebted to Peggy Bales, Jennifer Manley Rogers, Maurice Daniels, the Patricia Roberts Harris Fellowship, Damon Higgins, Robert Friedmann, Anthony Granberry, Rev. Archibald Killian, Sr., Geraldine Clarke, Albert Stokes, Harriet Collins, Samuel Wicks, O'Neal Fleming, and Ron James—all have lent their support, advice, and expertise.

I express special gratitude to Dr. Winfred M. Hope and my church family, Ebenezer Baptist Church, West, Athens, Georgia; Dr. I. L. Mullins, Sr., and my "home" church, First Missionary Baptist Church, Thomasville, Georgia; Rev. W. R. Wilkes, Jr., and McGhee Chapel AME Church, LaGrange, Georgia; all of my teachers and administrators of the Thomasville, Georgia, Board of Education; and my neighbors and community who were instrumental in my development.

CHAPTER 1

INTRODUCTION

Public services in both urban and nonurban areas, particularly their delivery and distribution, have a definitive affect on the community and are therefore important areas of public administration. Urban services involve the actual production, provision, and delivery of local governmental services (Sharp, 1990). These services consist of various governmental "line" and "staff" activities that are produced, provided, and delivered by local governments (Baer, 1985). Law enforcement is one major component of urban service delivery and undoubtedly one of the most crucial.

Urban service delivery has come under fire, scrutinized in the areas of bureaucratic efficiency and fiscal capacity (Fitzgerald & Durant, 1980; Bolotin, 1990). Such criticism has led to reduced general support for political institutions and public officials (Fitzgerald & Durant, 1980; Bolotin, 1990), increased privatization (Seader, 1986; Campbell, 1986; Rehfuss, 1986; Bennett & Johnson, 1981), and coproduction of public services (Brudney, 1986; Brudney & England, 1983; Whitaker, 1980). The assessment of citizen satisfaction with local governmental services and their delivery and distribution contributes toward the essential process of evaluating, restructuring, and implementing effective governmental policies. Citizen evaluations provide public officials with valuable feedback on community perceptions regarding the performance of local public agencies (Skogan, 1979).

Presently, citizen satisfaction with urban service delivery is mixed. In general the public views police and other municipal services positively within the United States. However, some dimensions of law enforcement are viewed less favorably (Rossi et al., 1974; Bloch, 1974; Hahn, 1971; Mladenka & Hill, 1978). This is especially true of crime and police-client relations within inner cities. Fear of crime continues to be a dominant theme that emerges from research on law enforcement. Various studies reveal that inadequate protection and service in predominately black neighborhoods rank as the most frequent complaint of citizens, particularly poor blacks (Wilson, 1975; Cooper, 1980; Radelet, 1986; Radelet & Carter, 1994). As a direct result of inadequate protection, police-client relations in poverty-stricken minority communities have suffered.

In the wake of this problem, police departments have examined and implemented new law enforcement strategies to establish and deliver more effective police services. Community policing is one example of new law enforcement strategy. Related to "coproduction" of police services (Koven, 1992; Whitaker, 1980), where citizens or clients who receive governmental services actively engage in individual or group action to assist or augment the eforts of service providers, this approach is both a philosophical and an organizational strategy designed to promote a new partnership of service delivery between people and police.

Although considerable research on citizen satisfaction with police services exists, little can be found that is specifically directed toward coproduction, a newly developed aspect of community policing. Assessing citizen satisfaction with local governmental services and proposals aids in evaluating, restructuring, and implementing governmental policies. Therefore, the perceptions and opinions of citizens on law enforcement require imperative analysis, particularly perceptions in inner city areas where residents have expressed pronounced concerns with unsatisfactory delivery of police services.

The implementation of a qualitative, nonexperimental research design using focus-group interviewing helped to collect, explore, and examine the perceptions and attitudes of East Athens residents and community policing officers assigned to the Nellie B and Vine community. The focus-group technique enabled the researcher to gather rich and in-depth data that also provided answers to the following three important questions: What expectations do inner city residents have for police services in general and community policing in particular? What helps to explain differing expectations? What are this implications for public administration?

Moreover, the important and relevant results from this study will not only benefit police service delivery and community policing policy efforts in East Athens but will also benefit universal efforts related to the implementation and evaluation of public policies.

CHAPTER 2

AN EXAMINATION OF
PREVIOUS RESEARCH

Urban services and delivery research highlights the problems of and alternatives to traditional approaches for delivering public services. Research on citizen satisfaction with urban services in general, and police services in particular, especially research on the relationship between race and citizen-initiated contacting and citizen satisfaction with public services, frequently unearths certain recurring themes. These findings have led to sustained scholarship on one alternative to public service delivery—community policing, that is, the coproduction of police services. This chapter focuses on a void in community policing research by studying African Americans' satisfaction with and perceptions of police and other urban services.

URBAN SERVICE DELIVERY

The public "represents, identifies, defends, and expresses the public interest—the will and the needs of the people and the services that they demand" (Seader, 1986:6). Therefore, local, state, and federal governments perform two important functions: they serve as mechanisms for reaching decisions about community and societal concerns and provide public goods and services (Savas, 1977).

5

Public choice theory, which applies economic reasoning to nonmarket decision making, analyzes the nature of goods and services. In *Comparing Urban Service Delivery Systems*, the authors distinguish between private goods, tool goods, common pool resources, and public goods based on the degree of exclusion and consumption of goods and services. Furthermore, *Comparing Urban Service* defines a public good "as one which is not subject to exclusion and is subject to jointness in its consumption or use" (Ostrom & Bish, 1977:7). However, other scholars caution and note that every act of public good has distributional effects, as not everyone will benefit equally (Jones, 1982; Goldwin, 1977).

Past limitations associated with the distribution of public goods have led to numerous alternatives or service arrangements for the provision and delivery of public services. Ruchelman (1989) and other scholars have identified numerous structural arrangements for delivering public services ranging from privatization to coproduction and from vouchers to volunteers (Savas, 1986). These structural arrangements have improved the provision and delivery of some public services, but have failed to rectify specific problems.

Four major areas associated with providing and delivering public services require monitoring: (1) efficiency—the amount of service provided based on the resources given (time, money, personnel) (Ruchelman, 1989); (2) effectiveness—the extent to which service objectives or goals are being met (Hatry et al., 1977); (3) equity, which includes equality of opportunity, market equity, or services proportionate to taxes paid and the distribution of benefits (Jones & Kaufman, 1974; Levy et al., 1974); and (4) responsiveness—the extent to which demands for services are being met (Ruchelman, 1989).

The particular delivery of urban services constitutes an important component of the public good, and is, therefore, susceptible to the aforementioned problems. As William Baer points out, urban (i.e., public, municipal, local) services consist of those which serve the public interest by accomplishing one or more of the following purposes: preserving life, liberty, and property; and promoting enlightenment, happiness, domestic tranquility and the general welfare. (1985:886)

Controversy exists on whether or not local governments must be involved in producing and providing urban services to the public. Some scholars note that urban services do involve the actual production, provision, and delivery of local governmental services (Valente & Manchester, 1984; Sharp, 1990). However,

> while local governments must be involved in the provision of services, production is not inherently a governmental task and can be accomplished through a number of mechanisms, depending on the type of service, the objectives sought, etc. (Brudney, 1986:11)

This assertion parallels others that emphasize structural arrangement alternatives in delivering public services (Savas, 1986; Ruchelman, 1989).

An important part of policy making and administration relates to the perennial political question of who gets what, when, where, how, and why (Lineberry & Welch, 1974; Jones et al., 1980; Laswell, 1958; Laswell, 1938). To develop a conceptual framework for the delivery of urban services, one must take into account the various existing service agencies and their service tasks. Additionally, one must be aware of the diversity of urban services as well as the sources of influence, content (mission or make-up of agency), and linkage (connection to power brokers or local politicians) (Nardulli & Stonecash, 1981).

Since bureaucratic agencies that reside in a nonneutral environment administer urban services, scholars have shown interest in the effectiveness of bureaucratic response as well as political influences on bureaucratic organizations (Nardulli & Stonecash, 1981). Scholars have also examined the spatial consequences of urban service delivery (Wolch, 1982), the political economy of urban service distribution (Rich, 1982), as well as a comparative analysis of urban service delivery systems (Ostrom & Bish, 1977). However, one central question has been constant: What rules are followed in deciding the distribution of urban services?

Service Delivery in the City proposes two models for the distribution of urban services: the urban-conflict model and the organizational model. The urban conflict model, which is synonymous with the political and class-bias model developed by Seung Jong Lee, emphasizes the competitive struggle among urban groups where local governments make policy and provide public services to those in need. In this model, which stresses political power and social class, the poor or the politically powerless are the clear losers. Although empirically supported by the works of Nardulli and Stonecash and Bolotin and Cingranelli, the research of Lineberry, Cingranelli, Boyle and Jacob, Antunes and Plumlee, Mladenka and Hill, as well as others refutes the validity of the urban-conflict model.

The organizational, or bureaucratic, model approached the problems associated with service delivery agency stability, a stability that affects interactions with its environment (Lee, 1994; Jones et al., 1980). The organizational model highlights the bureaucracy's standard operating procedures and is exemplified in the decision rules model outlined by Miranda and Tunyavong (1994).

Both the urban conflict model and the organizational model stress the development of routine service delivery rules for the provision of services. In turn, these models help to reduce or minimize intraorganizational conflict while defending the organization against outside critics; establish service agency goals in terms of the overall level of service (i.e., police services lead to crime reduction); and establish neutral goal-oriented service rules where distributional effects are a reality.

Still other scholars, arguing that both models are incomplete, suggest another model (Lee, 1994; Hero, 1986). This new, alternate model of urban service distribution, called "service type" highlights motivation and external influences to help explain the differential impact of the specific type of service on urban service distribution. As a result, Lee advances a new typology of urban services to explain how service types affect bureaucratic reactions to external influences, as well as the patterns of service distribution. Lee concludes

> that the basic tendency of bureaucracies in distributional decisions is to follow objective criteria guided by their blame-avoiding motivation. (1994:103)

Hence, objective criteria received priority as important determinants of the distribution of urban services whereas were variables associated with politics or class did not. Lee's model is supported in the research of Jones et al. (1978), Mladenka (1980), Mladenka and Hill (1978), and Boyle and Jacobs (1982).

Miranda and Tunyavong criticize the conventional wisdom in urban politics, namely that bureaucratic professionalism predominates urban service delivery and that systematic bias is unlikely to occur. In their "patterned equality" thesis, Miranda and Tunyavong argue that the importance of local politics in explaining urban service distribution has been underestimated. Therefore, they propose two politics-based models of urban service distribution: electoral coalition and regime maintenance (1994).

In their study of nearly two decades of funds for the allocation of Community Development Block Grants and capital improvement plans in the city of Chicago, Miranda and Tunyavong conclude that urban distributive policies are political. Therefore, the local politics models of electoral coalition and regime maintenance seem to provide a viable explanation of who gets what from city government. Therefore, the more a community politically supports their elected officials, the more favorable or preferential the distribution of services to that community, ward, or district will be (1994). These findings are consistent with the research of Rundquist and Ferejohn (1975), Browning, Marshall and Tabb (1984), and Stone (1989).

Unfortunately, methodological problems limit research on the distribution of public services as well. This includes urban services. Scholars identify three issues affected by such problems: (1) inadequate equity conceptualization in service distribution; (2) issues of what to measure in terms of resources, activities funded by the resources, outcomes, or changes in relevant social conditions (as well as difficulty packaging or measuring these things; and (3) and the units of analysis (Rich, 1982; Ostrom & Bish, 1977; Ruchelman, 1989). These limitations point out the difficulty of measuring and gaining a clear picture of the delivery of public goods. In particular, problems arise when trying to measure qualitative outputs by using quantitative methods. Therefore, evaluation methods that are applicable to the qualitative facets of some public services must be employed.

Unfortunately, inequitable delivery and distribution of public services is a reality, and this fact has led some scholars to argue for a pattern of urban service delivery and distribution that reveals the "compensatory fashion" or "responsiveness bias" of local governments (Schumaker & Getter, 1983; Rich, 1982).

Along this same vein, some research suggests considerable inequality of service delivery and distribution based on race (Brown & Coulter, 1983), and in suburban and smaller cities inequality exists based on heterogeneity and ethnic-racial segregation (Williams, 1980). Other research does, however, suggest a more equal distribution of neighborhood-oriented services regardless of race, politics, or socioeconomic status (Cingranelli, 1981; Lineberry, 1977; Antunes & Plumlee, 1977). Yet even seemingly equal distribution of urban services may mask unequal service delivery within certain neighborhoods and communities and may eventually contribute to citizen dissatisfaction.

CITIZEN SATISFACTION

Participation in America: Political Democracy and Social Equality, by Verba and Nie, defines political participation as "acts that aim at influencing the government, either by affecting the choice of government personnel or by affecting the choices made by government personnel." In their study, the authors target four modes of participation: voting, campaigning, communal activity, and particularized contacting. Truly, the traditional participatory acts of voting and campaigning, along with group or organizational activity, can directly influence the choice of government personnel and normally receive ample scholarly attention. However, Coulter notes the importance of citizen-initiated contacts with governmental officials, especially at the local level (1988).

In this era of municipal fiscal stress, bureaucratic corruption, and criticism, public dissatisfaction with government service delivery and distribution has fostered the emergence and development of citizen-initiated contacting studies (Sharp, 1982; Bachelor, 1984; Hero, 1986). In *Political Voice*, Coulter states that

> Citizen-initiated contacting reflects numerous problems that relate to a variety of municipal services. These problems and the services provided to alleviate them seriously affect the quality of life available to residents of each neighborhood in a city. (1988:15)

Therefore, citizens striving to influence the delivery of urban public services most regularly employ citizen-initiated contact, a form of communal activity (Jones et al., 1980). Moreover, these contacts hold significance because of their relationship to four vital aspects of democracy: citizen participation, representation, responsiveness, and distributional equity (Coulter, 1988).

Research on exactly who contacts local governments yields mixed results. A negligible correlation between socioeconomic status and citizen-initiated contact has been found (Mladenka, 1977; Hero, 1986; Jacob, 1972; Sharp, 1984). Their research, however, contrasts with the findings of Eisinger (1972), Sharp (1982), and Brown (1982), who discovered a positive linear relationship between SES and citizen-initiated contacting. Yet Coulter concludes that the theoretical assumptions that link SES and citizen-initiated contacting are not valid (1988).

In terms of need for public services, several studies found a negative linear relationship, where citizens of higher income areas tended to contact municipal governments less than lower income areas. In these cases, researchers presumed that lower SES meant greater needs for urban services, which in turn yielded a greater propensity to contact (Haeberle, 1986; Vedlitz, Dyer, & Durand, 1980; Burnett, Cole, & Moon, 1983).

Similarly, two additional models, the "the need-awareness" model and the "clientele need" model, also address the relationship between the need for urban services and citizen-initiated contacting (Coulter, 1988).

In Service Delivery in the City, the authors added political system awareness to a model that focused on the relationship between socioeconomic status and the need for public services. With regard to this, Coulter notes that as SES increases, awareness increases, need declines, and contacting increases to a certain point. Beyond that point, citizen-initiated contacting decreases, which results in a contact propensity that is greatest for middle SES and is lowest for lower and higher status residents of a community (Coulter, 1988). This curvilinear relationship has been supported by the findings of Bachelor (1984).

In his essay "Citizen-Initiated Contacts with Government Agencies," Thomas advances a clientele-need model that assumes no relation between socioeconomic status and need for services. Thomas also emphasizes that communities of different socioeconomic levels have different types of needs urban-service needs, and as a result they contact and become clients of different governmental agencies. Thomas's essay concludes that the need for governmental service is the primary factor in explaining citizen-initiated contacting, while SES is only a secondary factor. Other studies support Thomas's research (Dran & Smith, 1984; Brown, 1982).

Along the same line, Coulter (1988) examined the confusion and disagreement that characterized theories of citizen-initiated contact. In his research on the Mayor's Office of Citizens Assistance in Birmingham, Alabama, Coulter demonstrated that predominate theories of contact (i.e., SES and need-awareness theories) were inadequate; Coulter further concluded that citizens contact governmental agencies because they have a genuine need for those particular services (Coulter, 1988).

Concerning this general area of study, there also exists a large body of literature that examines racial differences in the propensity of citizens to contact urban and other governmental providers. This research suggests that: (1) no difference in black and white contacting rates is visible (Haeberle, 1986; Mladenka, 1977); (2) blacks contact at higher rates than whites (Thomas, 1982; Jones et al., 1977, Shin & Everson, 1980); and (3) whites contact at higher rates than blacks (Verba & Nie, 1972; Sharp, 1980; Jacob, 1972; Eisinger, 1972; Hero, 1986). The literature offers two explanations for the variance of perception: the inequitable distribution of public services to blacks and other minorities and the predominance of political participatory activities by whites (when compared to other racial populations).

In this regard, and with specific attention to this study, Coulter emphasizes that black disinclination to contact governmental agencies by stating

> Census tracts with a larger percentage of black residents tend to generate fewer contacts . . . it may be the low income of black residents, and not their race that inhibits their contacting. (1988:47)

Coulter also argues that a low level of African Americans contacting governmental agencies may be the result of either actual discrimination or African-American perceptions that contacting city government will yield little positive result, or both. All of the research on the relationship between socioeconomic status, race, and citizen-initiated contacting points compellingly toward the need to examine citizen satisfaction with and perceptions of urban services in communities consisting of poor minorities.

Even though blacks have been consistently more dissatisfied with local government services than whites (Aberbach & Walker, 1970; Durand, 1976; Brown & Coulter, 1983), citizen satisfaction with public services, such as of police, fire, parks and recreation, and sewers and streets services, has generally been positive. Four explanations of this phenomenon have been advanced (DeHoog, Lowery, & Lyons, 1990). These include: (1) individual-level explanations that focus on demographic variables (Aberbach & Walker, 1970; Schuman & Gruenberg, 1972; Durand, 1976; Brown & Coulter, 1983), community attachment and political attitudes or local political efficacy (Sharp, 1986; Brown & Coulter, 1983); (2) jurisdictional-level explanations that emphasize the dominant racial composition, average income level, local governmental system, actual level of services, and the actual quality of service in specific jurisdictions (Bish & Ostrom, 1973; Ostrom, 1976; Schuman & Gruenberg, 1972; Sharp, 1986); (3) city- and neighborhood-specific models that accent the uniqueness of different communities and suggest that urban leadership styles and management practices may impact citizen satisfaction with urban services (Yates, 1977; Swanstrom, 1985); and (4) hybrid individual-government models (DeHoog, Lowery, & Lyons, 1990) that find a meager account of satisfaction that emphasizes individual citizens' efficacy relative to local government and their attachment to their community, as well as the actual level and quality of services provided by local governmental entities.

In spite of some positive assessments, fiscal stress (Bolotin, 1990), public pressure (Sears & Citrin, 1982), and the negative public perceptions of government service (Fitzgerald & Durant, 1980) have contributed to reduced public support for local government institutions and/ officials, proven by negative citizen evaluations of municipal services (Durand, 1976; Fitzgerald & Durant, 1980; Christenson & Taylor, 1983). Service delivery and distribution inequalities, real or imagined, intensify the poor's disaffection toward local governments (Lineberry & Welch, 1974). Additionally, when the public questions the performance of a specific local governmental agency, namely its delivery and distribution of public services, disaffection toward the local government permeates the community (Beck, Rainey, & Traut, 1989).

Regarding the area of assessment of public service, Herbert Jacob (1971) urged scholars to look at one of the key services provided by local government, law enforcement. Police officers deliver to all citizens a spatially distributed service that aims at dealing with a large but finite set of social problems (Baker & Meyer, 1979). Many studies have examined specific citizen encounters with police in order to gauge the public's level of satisfaction (Bordua & Tifft, 1971; Frustenberg & Wellford, 1973). Sample surveys have been distributed in order to investigate the demographic correlates of perceptions of the police (Jacob, 1971; Hahn, 1971), identify the public's opinion of police policies (Boydstun, 1975), examine attitudinal correlates of different types of contact with the police (Walker et al., 1972), and evaluate the consequences or variation in the quality of service received by individuals who have summoned the police (Parks, 1976; Poister & McDavid, 1976).

More substantially, Brown and Coulter (1983) have developed a model of citizen satisfaction with police services based on the research of Marans and Rodgers (1975); Campbell, Converse, and Rodgers (1976); and Campbell (1981). According to Brown and Coulter, citizen satisfaction with law enforcement depends on their satisfaction with or assessment of the six different aspects of police services. These include police response time, police treatment of people, perceived equity of police treatment, perceived equity of police response time, perceived equity of police treatment of people, and perceived equity of amount of crime. As a consequence, public assessment of the different aspects of police service delivery hinge on the different characteristics of respondents, police services, and neighborhoods (i.e., demographics, political attitudes, neighborhood statistics associated with police service delivery, experiences with police service delivery, and expectations).

In their essay entitled "Subjective and Objective Measures of Police Service Delivery," a specific study of police services in Tuscaloosa, Alabama, Brown and Coulter conclude that citizen satisfaction with police services depends more on quick response time, fair and just treatment, and perceived equity of police services than the quantity or quality of services actually performed. In addition, Brown and Coulter note that the demographic variables of age, race, income, and education significantly relate to the three components of citizen satisfaction mentioned above (Brown & Coulter, 1983).

Additional research focuses on patterns of police and citizen perceptions of the police role (Rossi & Groves, 1970; Friedmann, 1992) as well as African-American (and other minority) perceptions of, and satisfactions with, police service delivery (Fogelson, 1968; Jacob, 1971; Hahn, 1971; Bloch, 1974; Cooper, 1980; Trojanowicz, 1982; Wilson & Kelling, 1982; Carter, 1983; Trojanowicz & Banas, 1985; Radelet, 1986; Jefferson, 1991; Chambliss, 1994). Although considerable evidence of positive citizen assessment of law enforcement exists, noticeable dissatisfaction with police services, especially in poor communities and on the part of African Americans and other minorities, should not be overlooked. In his essay published in *Urban Affairs Quarterly*, Steven Koven, predicts that "the time may be ripe for a more serious look at the concept of law enforcement coproduction" (1992:466).

COMMUNITY POLICING

Numerous scholars have proposed that the traditional conceptions of public service production and delivery have failed to recognize the importance of citizen input and the production capacities (e.g., neighborhood watches) of public consumers (Bish & Neubert, 1977; Percy, Kiser, & Parks, 1980). Some scholars argue that service production and delivery arrangements that include consumers or clients as participants will yield positive results, which in turn yield higher levels of satisfaction in citizen evaluations (Savas, 1986; Ruchelman, 1989; Whitaker, 1980). This practice of including citizens parallels the underlying philosophy of coproduction, an alternative for the provision and delivery of public services (Ruchelman, 1989).

Brudney and England define coproduction as "an emerging conception of the service delivery process that envisions direct citizen involvement in the design and delivery of city services with professional service agents" (1983:59). Similarly, Whitaker defines this alternative to public service delivery "as the active involvement of the general public and, especially, those who are to be the direct beneficiaries of the service" (1980:242). Whitaker further notes that this alternative "is especially important for services which seek transformation of the behavior of the person being served" (1980:246). Ruchelman adds, "Through the joint planning with service workers, and by performing a role in implementation, citizens are able to play an important role in the services they receive" (1989:33).

In his essay "Rebuilding the Public's Trust," William Ide asserts that community involvement and participation are key to breaking the current cycle of crime and violence. Many scholars note that coproduction can potentially supplement the labors of paid public officials with the efforts of citizen consumers and raise the quality and efficiency of municipal services (Rich, 1979; Brudney 1982; Wilson, 1981). Further research has been directed to specific coproduction-type strategies for dealing with crime and improving community safety (Bish & Neubert, 1977; Pennell, 1978; Percy, 1979; Percy, 1978; Sharp, 1978; Sharp, 1978).

Community policing is a corollary of the coproduction of law enforcement services. Specifically, community policing is an example of one of two types of coproduction, that is, citizens helping themselves (Brudney, 1986; Ruchelman, 1989). "In self-help programs, individuals or groups, often at the urging of local officials, undertake activities that either lie beyond government budgetary capabilities or extend existing service levels" (Brudney, 1986:11). This arrangement by local governments encourages individuals and groups such as neighborhood associations or communities to work directly and jointly with police officers (Ruchelman, 1986; Kiser & Percy, 1980; Percy & Baker, 1981).

Both a strategic concept and organizational strategy, community policing seeks to redefine the ends and means of traditional policing. Advocates argue that community policing, which seeks community involvement in the coproduction of law and order, will help increase the efficiency and effectiveness of police service delivery and distribution, even in times of scarce governmental resources (Walker & Walker, 1990; Brown, 1991; Trojanowicz & Bucqueroux, 1994). Although many dimensions of community policing parallel earlier policing strategies (foot patrol, beat cop, etc.), current proposals are rather sweeping and comprehensive (Vernon & Lasley, 1992; Lasley, Vernon, & Dery, 1995; Peverly & Phillips, 1993; Furguson, 1993; Fulwood, 1990).

Community Policing: How to Get Started defines community policing as a "philosophy of full-service personalized policing where the same officer patrols and works in the same area on a permanent basis, from a decentralized place, working in a proactive partnership with its citizens to identify and solve problems" (Trojanowicz & Bucqueroux, 1994:3). Research indicates that an effective partnership between community members and police play a deciding role in the reduction of crime and promotion of security. Foremost, community policing bases itself on this research (Skolnick & Bayley, 1986; Sparrow et al., 1990). It also reflects the conviction that contemporary problems or challenges facing law enforcement require full-service policing.

Full-service policing encompasses proactive and reactive law enforcement strategies that involve the community directly as partners in the process of identifying, prioritizing, and solving problems (Trojanowicz & Bucqueroux, 1994; Walker & Walker, 1990). Community policing underscores the fact that citizens are the first line of defense in the fight against crime and that effective crime fighting is based on cooperation, coproduction, and involvement and interaction of community institutions (Moore, 1992; Brown, 1992; Whitaker, 1990; Koven, 1992; Stewart, 1986; Tumin, 1986). Therefore, community policing closely associates with and is affected by shifts by police organizations from centralized, top-down-hierarchical, functional, organizational structures to decentralized, participatory, bottom-up, localized structures that encourage closer ties with surrounding communities (Moore & Stephens, 1991).

Community policing redefines the mission of the police to focus on solving community problems. Success or failure, then, depends on solving problems and not just processing arrests, writing tickets, and issuing citations (Trojanowicz & Bucqueroux, 1994). Community policing initiatives target to serve inner-city environments where concentrated crime and the unsatisfactory provision and delivery of public services exist. This innovative approach to policing directs urban service delivery toward the achievement of three goals: reducing crime and the fear of crime, improving service delivery, and improving quality of life. In addition to these instrumental goals, community policing is designed as an end in itself. As Mark Moore states in "Problem Solving and Community Policing," this form of policing "sees the community not only as a means for accomplishing crime control objectives but also as an end to be pursued" (1992:123).

In addition to redefining the mission of police, the idea of community policing also carries implications for police legitimacy, especially in its emphasis on the needs and desires of the community. As a result, community satisfaction and harmony become important bases of legitimacy along with crime fighting competence and compliance with the law. Politics, especially when defined as community responsiveness and accountability, reemerge as a virtue and an explicit basis of police legitimacy (Moore, 1992).

With particular relevance to police legitimacy, Susan Trojanowicz in *Theory of Community Policing* proposes that community policing is based on two social science theories: normative sponsorship theory and critical social theory. The normative sponsorship theory postulates that most people are of goodwill and will cooperate with others to facilitate the building of consensus (Sower, 1957). Critical social theory focuses on how and why people cooperate to correct and overcome the socioeconomic and political obstacles that prevent them from having their needs met (Fay, 1984). Enlightenment (education of the public), empowerment (public political activity), and emancipation (liberation through reflection and social action) form the three core ideals of critical social theory. These three ideals ensure that the more various groups share common values, beliefs, and goals the more likely they will agree on common goals when they interact for the purpose of improving their neighborhoods.

Normative sponsorship theory, critical social theory, and the basic characteristics of community policing help to justify the study proposed and its focus on African-American citizen assessments of law enforcement in general and community policing in particular.

As will be revealed in the following chapters, a systematic study of perceptions held by East Athens residents sheds light on the delivery of law enforcement services, particularly community policing. Furthermore, such a systematic study underscores the importance of assessing the values and effectiveness of general coproduction and urban service delivery.

CHAPTER 3

METHODOLOGY

The primary purpose of this study is to explore attitudes toward and perceptions of police services and community policing held by African Americans residing near or within the Iron Triangle neighborhood of East Athens, Georgia. A secondary and related purpose of the study centers on exploring the attitudes and perceptions of community policing officers assigned to the East Athens beat.

Athens-Clarke County, Georgia is a viable place to conduct research on citizen perspectives on community policing and the delivery of police services, because community policing scholars have speculated that the impact of community-oriented policing should be more apparent or pronounced in smaller cities and towns—locales where residents are still familiar with or cognizant of local police officers. Additionally, the community policing project in Athens-Clarke County is relatively new, and cannot be considered full blown under any criteria. The project under study here has only been partially implemented in the Nellie B and Vine neighborhood of East Athens. At that point and time, no other collection of feedback on the East Athens initiative had been made except for what is revealed here.

A qualitative, nonexperimental design using focus group interviewing was implemented to collect information about the perceptions and attitudes of East Athens residents and officers of the Athens-Clarke County Police Department. Focus group interviewing examines a range of perceptions, attitudes, and opinions on a given topic of discussion that is not designed to reach consensus (Morgan, 1988). By asking general and specific questions about police services and community policing and by providing a forum conducive to insightful response, this approach provides information on both clients' and officers' points of view and a basis for evaluating the consistency of opinion within and between these groups.

This chapter addresses five elements of methodology used throughout the study. First, the study site for the research will be described. Then, the basic research design will be specified, followed by the profiling of focus groups, discussion sites, and research expectations. After covering this ground, an overview of focus group interviewing will be provided. Finally, an overview of the analysis plan will be outlined.

STUDY SITE

Athens-Clarke County is a consolidated (city-county) government in Northeast Georgia, has a population of 87,594 citizens, and is the home of the University of Georgia (see Table 3.1). Athens-Clarke County, like many rural and urban areas across the nation, has experienced a dramatic increase in crime, violent crime, and illegal drug sales and use. All three of these factors increase community awareness and fear of crime. These difficult problems, especially the sale and use of illegal drugs and the destruction that follows, are most evident in Census Tract 3—East Athens.

Local authorities describe Census Tract 3 as "an open air drug market" that has been plagued by the crime and violence that accompanies illegal drug trade. The poorest census tract in Athens-Clarke County, Census Tract 3 has been the recipient of many governmental redevelopment and revitalization programs to help combat the inner-city-type problems its 6,119 residents face daily (see Table 3.2 and Fig. 3.1).

TABLE 3.1

DEMOGRAPHICS OF ATHENS-CLARKE COUNTY

Income		*Below Poverty Level*	
Median Household Income	$20,806	Below Poverty Level (All Persons)	27.00%
Percent < $10,000	26.12%	Children Below Poverty Level	26.20%
Percent < $15,000	38.13%	Female-Headed Households w/ Children < 18 years	51.95%
Percent < $50,000	82.26%	Female-Headed Households w/ Children < 5 years	69.52%
Median Family Income	$30,919	*Education*	
Per Capita Income	$13,631	< 9th Grade	5.03%
Population		9th to 12th (No Degree)	6.70%
Total	87,594	Total Without High School Diploma	11.73%
White	71.01%	High School Graduates	11.58%
Black	26.96%	*Unemployment*	
Asian	1.17%	Percent Employment in Service Sector	25.90%
Other	0.65%	Percent Unemployed (1989)	10.50%
Elderly (Over 65)	10.10%	*Households*	
Total Children	17,552	Total	33,113
Housing		Female-Headed Households with Children	2,524
Owner Occupied	44.21%	*Age*	
Renter Occupied	55.79%	Under 18	20.30%
Median Value	$72,100	18 to 24	20.20%
Median Gross Rent	$ 282	65 or Older	17.20%

Source: Athens-Clarke County Departments of Planning and Human and Economic Development.

TABLE 3.2
DEMOGRAPHICS OF CENSUS TRACT 3: EAST ATHENS

Income		Below Poverty Level	
Median Household Income	$12,411	Below Poverty Level (All Persons)	43.70%
Percent < $10,000	38.60%	Children Below Poverty Level	50.00%
Percent < $15,000	57.30%	Female-Headed Households w/ Children < 18 years	66.00%
Percent < $50,000	96.60%	Female-Headed Households w/ Children < 5 years	76.60%
Median Family Income	$16,429	Education	
Per Capita Income	$ 7,096	< 9th Grade	25.90%
Population		9th to 12th (No Degree)	26.40%
Total	6,119	Total Without High School Diploma	52.30%
White	33.40%	High School Graduates	26.00%
Black	65.00%	Unemployment	
Asian	1.10%	Percent Employment in Service Sector	25.90%
Other	0.50%	Percent Unemployed (1989)	8.60%
Elderly (Over 65)	9.50%	Households	
Total Children	1,552	Total	2,505
Housing		Female-Headed Households with Children	460
Owner Occupied	32.00%	Age	
Renter Occupied	68.00%	Under 18	25.40%
Median Value	$35,600	18 To 24	23.90%
Median Gross Rent	$ 329	65 Or Older	9.50%

Source: Athens-Clarke County Departments of Planning and Human and Economic Development.

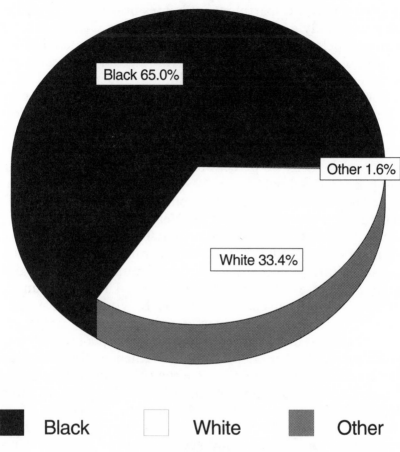

Black 65.0%

Other 1.6%

White 33.4%

■ Black ☐ White ▨ Other

FIGURE 3.1
RACIAL DEMOGRAPHICS OF CENSUS TRACT 3

Predominately a poverty-stricken black community, East Athens suffers from limited economic and educational opportunities and few other positive options for its residents (see Fig. 3.1). This community typifies many underclass neighborhoods in larger cities across America. The 1990 census data for East Athens indicates a median household income of $12,411 with a median family income of $16,429 and a per capita income of $7,096. Sixty-five percent of all residents rent the apartments or homes in which they reside. Approximately 44 percent of all who live in Census Tract 3 struggle below the poverty level. Children, female-headed households with children under the age of eighteen, and female-headed households with children under the age of five account for 50, 65, and approximately 77 percent of the population, respectively. Approximately 52 percent of East Athens residents have not obtained a high school diploma, and approximately 26 percent did not progress beyond the ninth grade. Only 26 percent of East Athens residents graduate from high school.

The Nellie B and Vine community, located in East Athens, consists primarily of the Nellie B public housing project and surrounding low-income rental housing. Very few residents of the Nellie B and Vine communities own their homes. Similar to other inner-city communities, local, legitimate businesses are almost nonexistent. The Iron Triangle, which is the intersection of Nellie B, Vine, and Fairview Streets, connects local businesses and contains a thriving and active open-air drug market. A liquor store, a pool room/sandwich shop, a barber shop, and a convenience store make up the businesses that directly serve the community. Many residents suspect that some of these businesses serve as store fronts for selling drugs and laundering drug profits.

The Athens-Clarke county government attempts to respond to the problems and needs of this community. Currently, a local economic redevelopment and revitalization project targets the Nellie B and Vine business community. This community also includes a satellite office of the Athens-Clarke County Human and Economic Development Department. Also, the Athens-Clarke County Police Department has implemented the East Athens community policing initiative designed largely to target the open-air drug market. Even though three police units serve the Nellie B and Vine community (zone patrol officers, public housing officers, and community policing officers), only the last of these three involve themselves in the community policing effort.

Part of a general movement in law enforcement that has

been sweeping the country for the past fifteen years, the East Athens community policing initiative has been interacting with the Nellie B and Vine community since November 1993. Although not fully implemented, the East Athens initiative is currently popular among officers involved. The East Athens Initiative consists of seven officers—one unit commander and six community policing officers. Initially, this group consisted of a white male unit commander, three black male officers, one black female officer, and two white male officers. At the time of the focus-group discussions, the unit was led by a black male and consisted of two white males and four black males. Headquartered in a neighborhood substation located within the Nellie B and Vine area, these officers directly interact with and serve the community.

Volunteers for this initiative were solicited by special departmental incentives—set shifts, days off, and a chance to take part in innovative law enforcement that serves communities in need. Although the new program geared itself toward black officers, no formal selection criteria were evident. Similarly, volunteers established a Community Leadership Council of local citizen leaders within the general Athens-Clarke County community. Although not formed to represent the targeted community, the Community Leadership council does advise the community policing initiative.

Start-up community policing training for the East Athens Initiative (EAI) was twofold: training of EAI staff and training for members of the Community Leadership Council. The unit commander received approximately twenty-six hours of start-up training that included a three-day course on community policing taught at the local police academy. This training consisted of a general overview of community policing and highlighted community coalition building, crisis intervention, crime suppression, and more traditional methods that are used in conjunction with this organizational strategy. Officers assigned to the EAI unit received eight hours of formal community policing start-up training as well as approximately eight to ten hours of informal training including foot patrol, coalition building, crisis intervention, and crime suppression. Since the focus group discussions, EAI officers have received additional community policing training. The Community Leadership Council received approximately six to eight hours of training. This training centered on a general overview of the philosophy of and approach to community policing.

No extensive departmentwide training of officers was provided. Officers not assigned to this initiative were given an informal and general overview of community policing. However, no specific, systematic training on their roles or their potential effect on this endeavor was provided. Similarly, there was no evidence that the ordinary citizens of the Nellie B and Vine community received preparation for the implementation of the EAI program.

BASIC RESEARCH DESIGN

In this study, a hybrid, clinical-phenomenological rather than exploratory approach to focus-group research was used. This approach allows the researcher to examine a set of participants who are not amenable to personal surveys or direct observations, in hopes of describing their respective experiences. This hybrid form is more applicable when the researcher or sponsoring agency is out of touch with the reality of targeted subjects, a situation that holds true in this case (Calder, 1977).

This research design and data collection method followed the structured protocol continuum in terms of questioning. In this, a sequenced set of questions pertaining to the issues of (1) community problems; (2) the level of trust and/or satisfaction with police services; (3) enlightenment, namely knowledge of the ideals of community policing; and (4) empowerment, that is, sociopolitical activity or community-suggested improvements that were used. A list of these questions is included in Table 3.3.

All questions were open-ended (i.e., a stimulus for respondents), thereby providing participants with the opportunity to give examples and to clarify statements. This for-

TABLE 3.3
FOCUS-GROUP INTERVIEWS

		Issues		
Groups and Questions	Community Problems	Level of Satisfaction/Trust	Enlightenment	Empowerment—Community Suggested Improvements
Elderly	Thinking back over the past three years, what are the major problems facing this community?	How do you feel about police services in East Athens? What would you like to see the police do?	Is the policing style in this community, the same as it was three years ago? How is it different?	Do you engage in any individual or group activities that seek to improve your community? What can or should the police do to provide better police services to residents of your community? Do you ever express to the police these suggestions?
Adults	Thinking back over the past three years, what are the major problems facing your community?	How do you feel about police services in East Athens? What would you like to see the police do?	Is the policing style in this community the same as it was three years ago? How is it different?	Do you engage in any individual or group activities that seek to improve your community? What can or should the police do to provide better police services to residents of your community? Do you ever express to the police these suggestions?

(continued on next page)

TABLE 3.3
(continued)

	Issues			
Groups and Questions	Community Problems	Level of Satisfaction/Trust	Enlightenment	Empowerment—Community Suggested Improvements
Teenage Males	Thinking back over the past three years, what are the major community problems on the Eastside?	How do you feel about police services in East Athens? What would you like to see the police do?	Is the policing style in this community the same as it was three years ago? How is it different?	Do you engage in any individual or group activities that seek to improve your community? What can or should the police do to provide better police services to residents of your community? Do you ever express to the police these suggestions?
Children	What are the best things about where you live? What are the worst things about where you live?	When do you see the police? What are they like?	Do you know the police officers who work in your neighborhood? How long have you known them? How would you describe what they do?	Do you or a group of your friends ever try to help the police solve problems? What do you think can help the police solve problems where you live?

(continued on next page)

TABLE 3.3
(continued)

			Issues		
Groups and Questions	Community Problems	Level of Satisfaction/Trust	Enlightenment	Empowerment—Community Suggested Improvements	
Officers	Thinking back over the past three years, what would you consider the major problems facing the East Athens community?	How do you think the residents feel about police services in East Athens? What do you perceive influences their viewpoint on police services?	How would you describe your job as a community policing officer?	What community groups do you come in contact with? What are their suggestions of community improvement? How do you feel about the level of community involvement in combating the problems facing this community?	
Follow-Up Questions to All Group	What are the new problems of the community? What are the old problems? What caused the new problems?	How do you feel about the police officers who work in this community? What makes you feel that way?	How would you describe the role of the police officer who works in this community? How would you describe the role that you have?	If you were in charge of making decisions on policing for your community, what would you do? Please list your priorities! Would your actions be the same as the officers or different? How?	

mat allowed the researcher to probe responses. The questioning sequence moved from more general questions to specific ones. This study aimed not to break away from research on citizen satisfaction but to apply a different methodology to its study, to explore and enhance the interpretation of quantitative results, and to add depth to the responses obtained in more structured surveys. The study used a descriptive interpretive technique to compare and contrast perceptions and attitudes within different demographic groups and with those officers assigned to a new community-policing unit.

FOCUS GROUPS, DISCUSSION SITES, AND RESEARCH EXPECTATIONS

In the Nellie B and Vine community, four major groups of African-American residents were assembled: the Elderly (56 years old and older); Adults (20 to 55 years old); Teenagers (13 to 19 years old); and Children (6 to 12 years old). A total of nine different groups of residents participated in focus-group discussions: Teenage Males I, Teenage Males II, Teenage Females, Teenage Male Juvenile Offenders, Female Children, Male Children, Female Adults I, Female Adults II, and the Elderly. No adult males participated in any focus-group discussions—those approached seemed skeptical of the research, apprehensive about cooperating, and unwilling to participate. With the exception of the elderly, all groups were homogeneous cohorts and consisted of between five and seven nonrelated individuals.

In addition to the aforementioned nine groups, the seven community policing officers assigned to the East Athens Initiative participated in the research as well. Five of the community policing officers assembled to create a focus group. Also, two one-on-one interviews further explored the perceptions of the supervising officer and another officer with whom the researcher had the most contact and interaction. These interviews served as a vehicle to gather information on how officers were assigned to the initiative, how officers were trained, and how the initiative was implemented.

The focus group interviews for residents, excluding the Teenage Male Juvenile Offenders, took place in several locations, including the East Athens Community Center in the Nellie B Community Building, an apartment located in the Nellie B public housing complex, Saint Mark's AME Church, and the East Athens Boys and Girls Club. The focus group participants frequently visit all of these East Athens locations during the week. The Teenage Male Juvenile Offenders discussion group took place in a conference room in the Clarke County Courthouse. The police focus group, as well as one of the interviews with community policing officers, took place at the East Athens Human and Economic Development satellite office. The other interview took place at a local restaurant, the Varsity, located outside of the East Athens community.

The researcher spent three months before the focus group discussions as a participant-observer in order to become acquainted with and gain entry into the community. It is not unusual for black inner-city residents, especially in drug-controlled areas, to show apprehension toward outsiders, particularly researchers. This skepticism increased when residents were asked to participate in discussions on law enforcement. To combat their apprehension, community leaders and officials of various local human service agencies (East Athens Community Center, East Athens Boys and Girls Club, Athens Housing Authority, Human and Economic Development Department, Athens-Clarke County Juvenile Court, Youth Detention Center, and St. Mark's AME Church) aided as consultants and served as contact persons to help identify potential citizen focus-group participants. The agencies involved offered recommendations on effective techniques or approaches to gain entry into the social structure and the trust of community residents. These agencies also helped to solicit volunteers for the aforementioned focus groups. This strategy patterned itself after the approach used by the Kettering Foundation in its unpublished research on the perspectives of South Central Los Angeles residents.

On the advice of the aforementioned community leaders, the researcher frequented the hang-outs and gathering places of the different targeted populations for three months. This included volunteering at the local community center and Boy's and Girl's Club, attending the local public housing tenants association meetings and functions, and worshiping at St. Mark's AME Church. These exhausting steps were required to gain the trust and acceptance of the potential targeted community residents.

Once the community seemed receptive, the researcher solicited potential participants via fliers and handbills for a general discussion on police services. Additionally, the researcher addressed members of the local tenant's association, parishioners of a local church, and residents of different age groups at the local community center and Boy's and Girl's Club in hopes of soliciting involvement. However, even after these efforts, most residents demonstrated little willingness to participate. Citizens who did volunteer to participate revealed a spirit of cooperation and therefore may not fully represent their community, as the majority of residents resisted participating, thereby perhaps implying a negative view of police services.

The contents of the handbills and fliers created and distributed by the researcher in order to solicit focus-group participants provided the groups with some idea of the research topic. Due to the controversy surrounding the equitable delivery of public services and consequential dissatisfaction and disaffection in poor, minority communities, the researcher expected a general skepticism and apprehensiveness on the part of community residents. Similarly, given the lack of political participation that has been found in many poor, African-American communities, little community involvement was anticipated. Nonetheless, female groups were expected to be more engaged, supportive, and active in the East Athens initiative.

AN OVERVIEW OF FOCUS-GROUP INTERVIEWING

Five fundamental assumptions provide the basis for focus-group research: (1) people are a valuable source of information; (2) people can report on and about themselves; (3) the facilitator, who focuses the interview, can help people retrieve forgotten information; (4) group dynamics can generate genuine information rather than establish a "group think" phenomenon; and (5) interviewing a group is better than interviewing an individual (Lederman, 1989). The focus-group research technique stemmed form the nondirective interviewing style characteristic of open-ended questioning. This style allows individuals to respond to questions without the interviewer setting boundaries or providing clues for potential response categories. Therefore, this method removes a significant amount of control and domination on the part of the researcher (Morgan, 1988; Krueger, 1988).

Focus-group research directs itself toward the concerns, needs, and feelings that underlie people's opinions and preferences. The nondirective interviewing method of focus groups begins with a limited set of assumptions and places considerable emphasis on getting in tune with the reality of the interviewee and seeing the world through their eyes (Krueger, 1988).

Focus-group techniques involve the use of in-depth group interviews in which participants are selected because they constitute a purposeful, but not necessarily representative, sample of a specific population (Stewart & Shamdasani, 1990). The focus-group interview also traces its roots to the use of basic group-therapy methods (Szybillo & Berger, 1979).

> Its conceptualization is based on the therapeutic assumption that people who share a common problem will be more willing to talk amid the security of others with the same problem. (Lederman, 1990:119)

Therefore, homogeneity is an important prerequisite for meaningful exploration of the topic of discussion (Axelrod, 1975).

Since its inception, focus-group interviews have been widely used in market research where the technique was adopted to address the limitations of standard, large polling techniques (Lederman, 1990; Cox, Higgonbotham, & Burton, 1976; Adler, 1979). In "Applications of Focus Group Interviews in Marketing," the authors note that mass surveys generate little insight into the reality of the marketplace (Cox et al., 1976). Therefore, the focus-group method attempts to explore people's perceptions, feelings, and behaviors. Currently, focus-group research has been effectively used in educational and social scientific research (Kolbert, 1992; Gamson, 1992; Harwood, 1991; Lederman, 1988). And as emphasized in qualitative methodology literature (Morgan, 1988; Krueger, 1988), focus groups help provide information to decision makers at three separate points in a particular process: before, during, or after a program or service is provided. Additionally, focus groups can be used in conjunction with quantitative methods. These connections include preceding quantitative procedures, simultaneously with quantitative procedures, after quantitative procedures, and independent of quantitative procedures.

Focus-groups provide a number of advantages relative to other types of research (Stewart & Shamdasani, 1990; Morgan, 1988; Krueger, 1988; Byers & Wilcox, 1992). The efficiency of focus-group interviewing allows the researcher to interact directly with respondents; focus-group interviewing also provides the opportunity to capture in-depth real-life data in large quantities and allows respondents to react and build on the responses of other group members. Additionally, the flexibility of focus groups make them an excellent tool for obtaining data from children, semiliterate or illiterate persons, or marginalized populations. Furthermore, focus groups provide comprehendible results (Stewart & Shamdasani, 1990; Morgan, 1988; Krueger, 1988; Lengua, Roosa, Schupak-Neuberg, Michaels, Berg, & Weschler, 1992). Specifically, focus-group research has been proven to provide a holistic understanding of the perceptions, experiences, and attitudes of poor African-American and other minority populations (Jarrett, 1993; Saint-Germain, Basford, Montano, 1993; Jenkins, 1995; D'Amico-Samuels, 1990).

Limitations to focus-group methods do exist, however

(Stewart & Shamdasani, 1990; Morgan, 1990; Krueger, 1988; Byers & Wilcox, 1992). The difficulty in assembling focus groups and the small number of participants significantly limit generalization to a larger population. The interaction of respondents within the focus-group setting may lead to "group think," domination by an opinionated member, or both. Furthermore, focus groups may be biased by the moderator (Stewart & Shamdasani, 1990; Morgan, 1988; Krueger, 1988). However, these drawbacks can be controlled by moderator awareness and objectiveness, specifically, by the moderator not providing cues about what types of responses and answers are desirable. This was achieved by controlling body movements, facial expressions, and voice inflections.

As emphasized earlier, there is a viable role for focus groups in social science research. In this respect, Byers and Wilcox (1991) have noted six appropriate inquiries for focus-group research. These include: (1) How do people interpret and respond to messages or message campaigns? (Lehman, 1987; Kolbert, 1992); (2) How might people resist organizational change? (Wilcox, 1988; Boden, 1989); (3) How can service be improved? (Boden, 1989; Barnett, 1989); (4) How will people respond to new technologies? (Wilcox, 1988); (5) How effective are training and evaluation methods? (O'Donnell, 1988); and (6) How should survey questionnaires develop? (Campbell & Fiske, 1959).

ANALYSIS PLAN

Researchers advance two basic approaches to analyzing focus-group data (Morgan, 1988). These include a strictly qualitative or ethnographic summary (Templeton, 1987) and a systematic coding via content analysis (Krippenndorf, 1980). Not mutually exclusive, these two approaches can be combined (Morgan, 1988). This study employs a combined ethnographic-content analysis approach, which enabled the researcher to describe focus-group discussions and interviews by directly quoting participants. Moreover, this allowed the researcher to count or code (i.e., using the numerical descriptions) the frequency of words and statements in the identification of group themes or perceptions.

The analysis of focus-group data includes two basic steps (Knodel, 1993; Seidel & Clark, 1984). First and foremost one must physically organize and subdivide the data into meaningful portions (a method synonymous with the cut-and-paste technique described by Stewart and Shamdasani [1990]). Then the interpretative process must begin, which determines the criteria for organizing or arranging the "textual" data into analytically useful subdivisions (Seidel & Clark, 1984; Knodel, 1993).

Following this procedure, all group discussions and one-on-one interviews were taped and transcribed. The data breakdown included a two-step process where each group discussion was divided into two categories (see Fig. 3.2). These categories consisted of the major incidents described by participants and their prevailing perceptions of police service delivery. From these experiences and incidents, certain themes emerged and were identified. The analysis process involved themes that surfaced in all groups and interviews.

A combined ethnographic-content approach guided the analysis of emerging incidents, themes, and issues. Two types of content analysis were used—semantical content analysis and sign-vehicle analysis (Webe, 1990; Krippendorff, 1980; Janis, 1965). Semantical content analysis classifies signs according to their meanings. This type of analysis may take three forms: designation analysis, which determines the frequency with which certain objects, persons, institutions, or concepts are mentioned; attribution analysis, which examines the frequency that certain characterizations or descriptors are used; and assertion analysis, which is a combination of designation and attribution analysis. In this study, assertion analysis was employed.

Sign-vehicle analysis classifies content according to the psychophysical properties of signs, that is, counting the number of times a specific word or types of words are used (Stewart & Shamdasani, 1990). To get a more intimate feel for the data collected, a manual approach to capturing the content

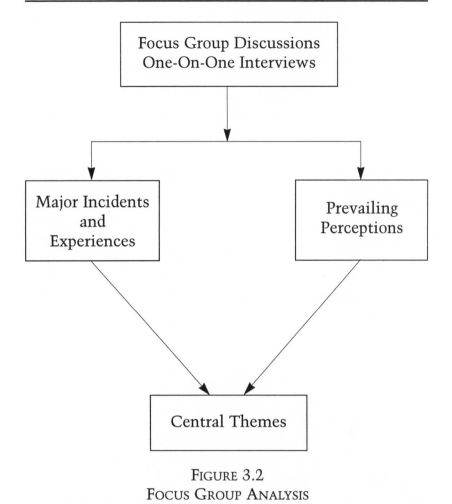

FIGURE 3.2
FOCUS GROUP ANALYSIS

and context of group discussions was used instead of a Key-Word-in-Context (KWIC) computer-assisted approach. All of these strategies are consistent with analytic strategies for qualitative data (Patton, 1990).

Finally, a descriptive-interpretive approach was used in place of a theory-building approach. In this approach one compares answers to questions across groups. This allows the researcher to compare and contrast perceptions, attitudes, and opinions within the different demographic groups of clients, as well as officers. This aided in the identification of common themes, statements, preferences, and viewpoints of groups and their respective participants. In short, this approach allowed the researcher to focus attention on how citizen groups were similar and how they differed in terms of their perceptions and attitudes toward police services in general and community policing in particular.

CHAPTER 4

A DESCRIPTIVE PROFILE OF FOCUS-GROUP DISCUSSIONS

Although no hypothesis was quantitatively tested, some propositions were considered in the analysis of discussion transcripts. The researcher projected community disaffection, apprehension, and skepticism, as well as a lack of community involvement by East Athens residents in the new community-policing endeavor. Yet, similar to the findings on community participation, females were envisioned to be more supportive of and involved in the East Athens initiative. These projections relate to four major issues: (1) community problems; (2) the level of trust or satisfaction with police-service delivery; (3) knowledge of the ideals of community policing; and (4) sociopolitical activity/community-suggested improvements. The first two deal with perceptions related to police-service delivery more generally, while the last two are particularly related to community-policing efforts. These issues were examined in the focus group interviews with residents and patrolling officers.

This chapter records the general responses of the focus groups and participants. The differences among groups on certain issues will be highlighted and some comparisons to relevant studies will be made. To conclude, relevant themes will be identified and analyzed in chapter 5.

PERCEPTIONS OF POLICE SERVICES

Community Problems

A series of questions was asked to all groups about their perceptions of community problems facing East Athens. Additionally, in follow-up questions participants were asked to identify old and new problems of the community, causes of these problems, and community needs; and the teenage and children's groups were asked about the best and worst aspects of living in their community. Table 4.1 summarizes the responses of the focus groups as they relate to community problems.

All residential focus groups and police officers, conceded that drugs and related drug-induced behavior (i.e., violence, shootings, loitering, high crime, etc.,) were and are the major problems facing East Athens.

> Drugs . . . it's a lot of drugs . . . People who sell drugs . . . Drugs is the main reason for the majority of every violent crime . . . is the cause for violent crimes, robbing people for money, armed robberies . . . breaking into your house, stealing VCRs and TVs. This is the root of it all and it's not being addressed as severely as it should.

Teenage Males I group and the Female Children group expressed similar sentiments. However, they also emphasized that these problems were particularly acute with teenagers.

> Teenagers are getting involved with drugs and killing each other for them. . . . A lot of people are in the drug scene. . . . Most teens too are in marijuana and stuff. . . . Most of them are selling it, mostly teenagers. . . . I see it like, the reason why it comes in sometimes because most of the teens our age see all this stuff, like shoes and clothes and stuff. They want to get it and they just need the money to buy it. And they know they ain't gonna get it no other way so, some of them go out and sell drugs.

TABLE 4.1
COMMUNITY PROBLEMS

Focus Groups	New and Old Problems	Causes of Problems	Community Needs	Rating of Community
Teen Males I	New: Teens and drugs Old: Violence	Increase in drugs; peer pressure, commercialism and materialism	Better response time, expanded police presence, drug- and violence-free places	High community rating when compared to the Westside (i.e., better schools; more activities; less public housing, drugs, and violence)
Teen Males II	New: Drugs Old: Violence	Lack of respect, failure of parents, the desire of money, to impress others	Respect from cops, better protection, removing drugs from community	High community rating when compared to Westside (i.e., more facilities, activities, and less violence)
Teen Female	New: Killings & shootings Old: Drugs	No suggestions	Better response time; more officers and expanded police presence	Best: friends, activities Worst: drugs, killings, violence

(continued on next page)

TABLE 4.1
(continued)

Focus Groups	New and Old Problems	Causes of Problems	Community Needs	Rating of Community
Teen Male Juvenile Offenders	*New:* Guns, drugs, violence *Old:* Fights, lack of role models	Addiction to drugs; a need for protection	Better response time, better protection, role models, activities for teens, to abolish curfew	"Ain't no best thing"
Female Children	*Problems:* Teens involved with drugs, violence, shootings	No suggestions	More patrolling officers, caring officers, officers doing a thorough job	*Best:* Friends, family, officers walking around the community *Worst:* violence and shootings
Male Children	*Problems:* the police, outsiders who deal drugs, and violent people and bullies	No suggestions	Caring officers, stopping the drug trade, protection from officers, more officers, disseminating cops	*Best:* activities and facilities *Worst:* Police, "bad people," and "the way people treat you"

(continued on next page)

TABLE 4.1
(continued)

Focus Groups	New and Old Problems	Causes of Problems	Community Needs	Rating of Community
Elderly	*New:* drugs & related activity *Old:* lack of services and infrastructure	*New:* "weakness," lack of training, despair	For officers "to do the same thing they been doing"	High ratings based on comparing current services to past services
Female Adults I	*New:* drugs, unruly children, child-abuse laws *Old:* drugs, alcohol, cops too friendly to criminals	*New:* "Parents not taking responsibility for their children"	Quicker response time, more respect from officers	No rating

(continued)

TABLE 4.1
(continued)

Focus Groups	New and Old Problems	Causes of Problems	Community Needs	Rating of Community
Female Adults II	New: Kids killing kids Old: Drugs, alcohol, domestic violence	Irresponsible parents, lack of community parenting, child-abuse laws, parents deviating from successful parenting methods of the past	Officers who are more involved w/in the community, quicker response time, respect from officers, parents to accept their responsibilities and the involvement of more community residents, increased anonymity in reporting crime, 24-hr patrols	No rating
EAI Cops	New: Drugs and its related activity Old: marijuana, alcohol	Lack of positive role models, lack of activities for juveniles	More structured activities for juveniles; positive role models; support from police administration, local, state, and federal government; and court system reform	Best: churches, East Athens Community Program, Nellie B Tenants Association Worst: Drugs and its related behavior

(continued)

TABLE 4.1
(continued)

Focus Groups	New and Old Problems	Causes of Problems	Community Needs	Rating of Community
EAIEP	*New:* Hidden drug market, illegitimate business owners *Old:* drugs, public intoxication, open-air drug market	Lack of skills, community apathy, lack of support from local government	Structured activities for juveniles, community involvement, increased local, state and federal support, university support, legitimate businesses	*Best:* Religious community, East Athens Housing community, Nellie B Tenants Association *Worst:* Drugs, alcohol, apathy of community
EAISCH	*New:* drug market, establish a rapport w/kids *Old:* community apathy	Lack of structured activities for juveniles, poverty which "causes some juveniles and parents to compromise their principles" for monetary gain and economic stability	More involvement and cooperation from community; structured activities for juveniles; more proactive local govt.; reformation of justice (juvenile) system	*Best:* Religious community, particular residents *Worst:* Drugs, community apathy

Police officers in the East Athens Initiative also expressed similar concerns:

> For instance, like there are a lot of kids selling drugs. From what I have found out from checking on the past is that a lot of drug dealers who have actually gone out and recruit kids sixteen and under to sell drugs for them for a small profit because they know if they got caught, never mind the juvenile system because they aren't going to do anything to them. . . . A lot of these experienced drug guys use these younger guys because they know they can get away. . . . You had this one particular instance where this kid, honestly wasn't but thirteen years old. We didn't know at the time but through investigation found out he wasn't but thirteen years old. [He] was running up to the undercover's vehicle and could barely get his head over the door with a handful of rock to sell it.

A related concern, Teenage Male Juvenile Offenders and East Athens Initiative officers emphasized the lack of positive role models as a community problem. Participants within the juvenile offender group also called attention to the need for positive role models and argued that ironically, within their community, dope dealers often fill this void and are surrogate role models for area youngsters. Drug dealers often possess the "nicest cars" and other material things that attract the attention of kids and adolescents. East Athens Initiative officers argued for more positive role models and fewer drug dealers.

Female Adults II group struggled with domestic abuse, teenage pregnancy, and a lack of parental support along with drugs as the major problems facing their community. Participants recounted incidents of domestic abuse that they had witnessed or were part of.

> There was another lady whose daughter's boyfriend . . . threatened the daughter. And I had a neighbor whose

house would be locked and the man somehow could take her window pane out . . . and come into her apartments, and be standing there waiting on her and jump on her. And the police, when they would come, would not take him away. They would walk him down to the car, talk to him, pat him on the back and let him walk on. . . . Well . . . last night, my ex-boyfriend . . . he climbed up to my top window . . . when I woke up, he was standing over me and my kids. This is the second time he'd done this.

Additionally, participants suggested teenage pregnancy as one of the main problems facing the community. They also identified preteenage pregnancy as a problem within the East Athens community. According to these group members, parents have abandoned the "old ways" of raising and rearing children. This results in a lack of parental backbone in disciplining children. However, group members did acknowledge that parents are not allowed to be disciplinarians because of current child-abuse laws. Therefore, group members advocated combining the "old ways" with forms of community parenting. In this regard, members recognized the need within the community for more parents to allow other adults to correct and give guidance to community youngsters.

The officers of the East Athens Initiative depicted lack of community involvement and the lack of community cooperation as major problems facing the East Athens community. Officers insisted that the entire community needed to be more involved and cooperative, asserting this as the only way to solve community problems. This sentiment, echoed by participants in the Adult Female II group, parallels research on successful community policing (Miller & Hess, 1994; Trojanowicz & Bucqueroux, 1994). These participants recognized that as citizens and neighbors within the East Athens community, they have not been as supportive as needed in aiding officers in solving community problems, admitting "We see things but we won't speak."

A one-on-one interview with a patrol officer identified

another community problem—the need to build an amicable partnership between police and citizens, especially a positive relationship between juveniles and police within the East Athens community. The officer emphasized that building a viable and nonadversarial relationship with juveniles in the East Athens community should be an organizational goal of the police department. Relatedly, he advocated expanding the East Athens Initiative to include the entire East Athens community.

SATISFACTION WITH POLICE SERVICE DELIVERY

A series of questions was asked to groups to gauge their level of satisfaction with police services and delivery. These questions asked residential participants to express their feelings on police services in East Athens, their personal expectations for police service delivery, and their satisfaction with police services in East Athens. Similarly, East Athens Initiative officers were asked about their perceptions of how residents feel about police service delivery in East Athens, their perceptions of the causes for the residents' perspective on police service delivery, and their personal expectations for police service delivery in East Athens. The general responses of the focus groups on these items are summarized in Table 4.2 and considered in the following sections.

All residential groups, with the exception of the Elderly focus group, were dissatisfied with the level of police services and delivery. This parallels previous research on race, age, and satisfaction (Campbell et al., 1976; Jefferson, 1991; Thomas & Holmes, 1992). The general cause for dissatisfaction largely focused on the slow response time of officers when called to crime scenes or incidents. These findings are consistent with earlier "traditional" and community policing research (Block, 1974; Frustenberg & Wellford, 1973; Pate et al., 1976; Trojanowicz, Steel, & Trojanowicz, 1986). Slow response time served to intensify citizen disaffection with local government service and parallels previous, social science research (Lineberry & Welch, 1974). Members of the

Teenage Males I group summed up this discontent by expressing a major incident that touched close to home.

> Sometimes, like when a murder and people call and they be serious, they wait. I mean, it seems like they take their own time and . . . They do!! They do take their time because when my cousin got killed, they didn't come to about twenty-five to thirty minutes later. And the ambulance didn't come to about thirty minutes after the police got there. . . . They could've saved his life.

Members of the Teenage Males II group, Teenage Male Juvenile Offenders, and Teenage Females expressed similar sentiments.

> Man, they ain't doing nothing. . . . They ain't doing nothing because, like, something happens, say somebody gets shot. It takes forever to come over here, like they are scared or something . . . [Officers] be around when you don't need them, but when you need them, they can't be no where to be found . . . they are lazy. They never come when they are supposed to.

Negative experiences, or police-citizen contacts that leave a nasty taste in the mouth of participants, family members, and friends also contributed to general dissatisfaction with police services and lack of trust by some residential focus groups. Members of the Teenage Male Juvenile Offender group related two such incidents that epitomized this dissatisfaction.

> They caught me up town after somebody had robbed somebody. . . . They pulled all of us over and just checked me down. Then they grabbed me by the thumb and put the handcuffs on, set me in the back seat. . . . So when they couldn't find nothing, they got mad. Then they tried to make like we had something. They took us up town and made us walk home.

TABLE 4.2.
SATISFACTION WITH POLICE SERVICES

Groups	Feelings on Police Services	Personal Expectations of Service Delivery	Rating of Police Services
Teen Males I	Dissatisfied—slow response time	Quicker service delivery; arrest and rehabilitate crack addicts	Low ratings based on slow response time
Teen Males II	Dissatisfied—slow response time, lack of respectful service	Officers to try harder, quicker response time, more respect shown, greater effort in getting drugs off the streets	Low ratings—cops aren't doing enough, and need for more officers
Teen Female	Dissatisfied—socioeconomic-based service delivery, fear of officers of black neighborhood	Quicker response time, more officers with increased presence, equitable service delivery regardless of socioeconomic status	Low ratings—slow response, lack of presence in community, and perception of socioeconomic-based service delivery
TMJO	Dissatisfied—slow response time, race-based service delivery, crime based service delivery	Quicker response time, no harassment by officers	Low ratings—slow response time, harassment, and perception of crime and race-based service delivery

(continued on next page)

TABLE 4.2
(continued)

Groups	Feelings on Police Services	Personal Expectations of Service Delivery	Rating of Police Services
Female Children	Dissatisfied—lack of officers intervening in situations, perception of officers not caring	Officers to intervene in situations that may escalate into violence, "more caring police"	Mixed ratings—some suggested that officers are present and active in the community, others stressed that officers tend not to care
Male Children	Dissatisfied—negative experiences of all participants except one, slow response time	For officers to be "nicer," to dismantle the drug trade, no harassment or false arrests	Low ratings by all participants except one; slow response time, prejudiced officers, lack of community involvement
Elderly	Very Satisfied—high service provisions based on past experiences	For officers "to do the same thing they been doing" since the implementation of EAI	High rating—increased service delivery and police presence
Female Adults I	Dissatisfied—slow response time, lack of respect, police organizational structure crime-based services, negative experiences	Quicker response time, better service delivery, increased police presence in community	Low ratings—slow response time, officer lack or respect for residents; crime-based service delivery

(continued on next page)

TABLE 4.2.
(continued)

Groups	Feelings on Police Services	Personal Expectations of Service Delivery	Rating of Police Services
Female Adults II	Dissatisfied—slow response time, lack of anonymity, police organizational structure, negative experiences, lack of respect; satisfaction with initial experience of new SGT and one EAI cop; socioeconomic-based service delivery	Quicker service delivery, equitable treatment, increased visibility of officers, respect from officers and anonymity of residents, nonjurisdictional officers	High ratings for EAI officers and new SGT, to housing officers because of their responsibility in maintaining peace in all public housing developments Low ratings—in police structure and organization

(continued on next page)

TABLE 4.2
(continued)

Group	Residents' Perception	Causes of Perception	Personal Expectations
EAI Cops	Generally satisfied with services	Satisfied—based on the past and present actions of residents Dissatisfied—due to the generalization of officers	To get back in touch with community, more supportive and involved residents, to expand COP program countywide
EAIEP	Generally satisfied with services	Satisfied—with switch to community policing and quicker response time	To increase level of community interaction, to expand COP program, to receive aid from local, state, and federal governments, as well as university community
EAISCH	General satisfaction with services but dissatisfaction may be present	Satisfied—based on the past and present actions of residents Dissatisfied—based on level of minimal community support and distrust based on the years of inequitable service delivery	To win back the trust of the community, cooperation from all aspects of community, to fairly distribute services in an equitable manner, increased interaction between officers and residents

> The police tried to rough me up, tried to rough me up . . .
> I had to put it on them. . . . I slammed him against the
> wall, he came back and put a little chin lock on me. I fell
> down to the floor and turned over on him, shot him a
> couple of 'bows. He called in backup and all of them
> piled in on me and started kicking me. One pulled out
> his blackjack and hit me across the head one time. . . .
> Then they just put me on in the car.

The first incidence holds significance because it happened
beyond the community boundaries of East Athens. A particularly powerful recollection for one focus group member, it added
to the general perception of how people from the East Athens
area are treated by police officers throughout Athens-Clarke
County. Both incidents highlight and legitimize East Athens residents' distrust of and dissatisfaction with police officers.

The Male Children group, like the Teenage Male Juvenile Offender group, also displayed dissatisfaction with police
services and expressed a general distrust of officers. This dissatisfaction was based on their own negative experiences or
on having witnessed the negative experiences of others, particularly family members or friends.

> There is only three things I dislike. I don't like the
> policemen because they are lowdown, bullies who try to
> fight you all the time, and the way people treat you . . .
> Low down is like when police try to be your friend one
> minute and then try to fight you the next minute . . .

> They are crazy . . . 'cause them white police just ride
> around like this and there is this one white boy. That's
> the one who twisted my other cousin's arm. . . . *they are
> just stupid!!!* Coming around locking people up for noth-
> ing . . . I bet if I saw somebody in their family doing
> drugs, I want to see if they would lock them up . . . They
> just come by and lock black people up.

> What they did to my momma one time, because a car
> had hit my momma's Honda, right. So she got mad and

started cursing. So the police said something to her. So she cursed the police out and they locked her up. But she got out that night. . . . See, that is stupid!!!

One day we were walking to the store at about nine o'clock that night and the police stopped us. And when they got out of the car, we took off running. . . . They stopped us for no reason. I wasn't fixing to stay around and get locked up, so I took off running.

Female Adult Groups I and II called attention to slow response time and to the police structure in the East Athens community. Participants indicated that jurisdictional arrangements associated with multiple police units were confusing. Both groups expressed unhappiness with the structure, organization, and distinction of the different police agencies that work within their community (the mix of public housing officers, zone police officers, and community police officers).

We call in for a policeman and the policemen that work in this community are not available, they tell us that they do not have any housing officers on duty. If they can work in other communities, why can't others come to this community and work?

Another problem with the police is there are seven officers assigned to public housing in all of Athens. If you get a call, you're only gonna get them. So if they're on Broad Street, you'll have to wait. There's an officer sitting right over here, but if he's not assigned, he ain't coming. You're only getting a housing officer. . . . We don't want just a public housing officer. We want a police officer [to respond to any and all calls]. We don't care where they have to come from.

On their car it says to serve and protect. . . . There shouldn't be no such thing as a housing police. They should all be like you say, to serve and protect whoever the individual . . . [may be].

The female adult groups expressed particular dissatisfaction with the East Athens Initiative's limited scope, its concentration around "the Block" area, and the fact that few officers get out and meet community residents.

> I asked her [CEO Gwen O'Looney], Why did you bring the cars back in the substation if they can't work with housing authority also . . . What was the point of bringing them back over here if they can't work in Nellie B too? . . . They are just out here for the drug patrol.

Additionally, both female adult groups were dissatisfied with what they see as a lack of respect that officers have for residents of the community. This parallels earlier research on dissatisfaction with police and other local governmental services (Jacob, 1971; Hahn, 1971; Rossi et al., 1974; Fogelson, 1968). Participants emphasized their conviction that the lack of respect that officers have for the community leads to unsatisfactory police service delivery.

> They look down on us because we stay in housing. We are just the same as the people way over on the other side, at Five Points. We are just as good as them. . . . If our policemen, as they put it, can go there, why not they come here when we need them? . . . I have called a policeman, without naming names or nothing, I have called a policeman. I called the police twice and told them to come out here and this was a domestic problem and loitering problem and I don't know if they ever came because I got tired and went to bed.

In contrast to other groups, the Elderly focus group expressed an extremely high level of satisfaction with police and other local governmental services. This rather atypical satisfaction was based on their comparisons of the delivery of community services in the past to those of the present. On average, each of these participant has lived in the community for over thirty-two years. In discussions, they all stated that police service delivery is much better than it was . . . They be patrolling up and down the street and they be watching and checking on things around here. . . . Three years ago, you couldn't find one police around here. . . . If you called the police three years ago, one may come. But now, three, four, and five show up. . . . It used to be so bad with dope where people couldn't sit out on the front porch . . . the women couldn't come out. . . . Now if you call, the police comes. You know, they didn't always used to come. . . . And now you can see them walking at night.

In addition to general satisfaction with police services, these residents expressed support for the East Athens Initiative. This seemed to derive from the initial experiences that some group members had with the East Athens Initiative sergeant and with one officer in particular. These positive experiences appeared to disseminate throughout the community and illustrate the importance of officer commitment to community policing. This parallels current community policing literature (Brown, 1991; Brown, 1992).

[The new Sergeant] got out and met the neighborhood, and he met the people who live in the neighborhood. He told each one of those neighbors, the people who live in Nellie B, "If you have a complaint about any officer that is out here, I will be in that office. If not, leave a message and I will come back to you." One somebody left a complaint about one of his officers. He went up to that person who had the complaint, with that officer, to take up that complaint and find out what was the problem and how did it get started. But, they got it straightened out. I have to give that man credit, he works with his officers along with the neighborhood.

They have a Hispanic name Eric who gets involved with the community. He came over and he went out and met most of the residents that's around here. When kids go into the store and they don't have money, he asked them, "What are you guys doing in the store?" . . . They said, "We want some ice cream." He asked them if they had any money. They said "No." . . . He said, "go and get your ice cream. I am going to pay for it this time, but don't come to the store unless you got money."

Officers interviewed thought that the community's satisfaction with police services and delivery was increasing. Their perception of the community's satisfaction was based on the evident friendliness of community residents, especially when compared to the actions of community residents in the not so distant past.

Residents are real receptive, as far as throwing their hands up [waving]. I think they feel more comfortable now with talking to the police, not like in the past. If the police officer pulled up and someone were to come over to the car, then some of the drug dealers or some of the people that were in criminal activities would consider them to be a snitch. But now, it's not unusual for everybody to come up and speak, both young, old, middle aged, male, female.

Additionally, officers argued that increasing the community's satisfaction with police services may be due to their partial success in dismantling the drug trade within the "Iron Triangle/The Block." Other factors contributing to improving citizen satisfaction include the change to community-oriented policing, quicker response time, and community cooperation and involvement.

Now there is somewhat more cooperation than there used to be. The fact that some people will openly tell you things. Some will, per se. They'll tell you but they'll call you on the phone or something like that. . . . Some people will come right on up now and they don't mind who see you talking to them, see them talking to you.

Interestingly, officers concluded that residents' dissatisfaction with police service delivery and distrust of police were the result of years of inequitable service delivery. Relatedly, they emphasized that this dissatisfaction is and will continue to change slowly with the new policing style.

> All those things have really hurt the police image and it is just hard trying to build it back up . . . it's a stereotype that we all have together as police officers. They see that uniform and they see this one person. Regardless of who the officer is, that's all they see is that uniform. . . . So it's going to take actually community-oriented police programs and actually getting together with the community to get it back to where it should be—to really kind of trust each other.

PERCEPTIONS RELATED TO COMMUNITY POLICING

Enlightenment

A series of questions was put to all groups to measure their general knowledge and understanding of the ideals of community policing. Specifically, participants were asked if they knew the EAI community officers; if they knew the role of a community policing officer; if the policing style in East Athens has remained constant or has it changed, if so, how, and what, if any, is their role as community residents in community policing. Likewise, East Athens Initiative officers were asked to gauge their level of interaction with community residents, to define community-oriented policing, as well as their role as a community policing officer, to compare and contrast the old policing style or structure with the current one, and to depict the resident's role in community oriented policing. The general responses of the focus groups, as they relate to these issues of enlightenment are summarized in Table 4.3 and considered in the following sections.

In general, most residents expressed a lack of direct knowledge of, or contact with, East Athens Initiative officers. This obviously contrasts with research on the requirements of community policing, research that highlights the impor-

TABLE 4.3
ENLIGHTENMENT: KNOWLEDGE OF IDEALS OF COMMUNITY POLICING

Groups	Knowledge of Community Officers	Role of EAI Officers	Policing Style	Residents' Role
Teenage Males I	No personal knowledge.	Described as sitting or hanging around the Block.	Can detect difference in style with the increased number of officers.	Roles were mentioned, yet no role in aiding officers.
Teenage Males II	No personal knowledge.	Described as hanging out or patrolling Block area.	Detect difference with increased number of officers and foot patrols.	Lack of role based on fear of retribution.
Teenage Females	No personal knowledge of EAI officers. Knowledge of housing officers.	Described as protecting the public, halting drug trade.	Didn't express or detect a change, but were cognizant of substation.	Roles were mentioned but lack of role in aiding officers due to fear of retribution.
TMJO	No personal knowledge of EAI officers. Knowledge of some housing and patrol officers.	Described as patrolling Block area.	Can detect difference based on police presence in Block area. Described style as "rougher" or more aggressive.	No role in aiding officers.

(continued on next page)

TABLE 4.3
(continued)

Groups	Knowledge of Community Officers	Role of EAI Officers	Policing Style	Residents' Role
Female Children	Lack of personal knowledge of EAI officers.	Described as "helping out residents" and "watching over neighborhood."	Didn't express or detect a change, but were cognizant of substation.	Lack of role in aiding officers, however one participant acknowledged that all residents should have a role.
Male Children	Lack of personal knowledge of EAI officers. Only 1 participant acknowledged knowing any officer.	To protect community residents.	Didn't express or detect a change, but were cognizant of substation.	Expressed no role and no interest in aiding cops, with only one dissenting. Also expressed fear of retribution.
Elderly	Lack of personal knowledge.	Described as patrolling community.	Can detect a change due to increase in service delivery and police presence.	To built a rapport with younger generation and limited involvement with police due to fear of retribution.

(continued on next page)

TABLE 4.3
(continued)

Groups	Knowledge of Community Officers	Role of EAI Officers	Policing Style	Residents' Role
Female Adults I	Lack of personal knowledge of EAI, yet some knowledge of housing and zone officers.	Described as hanging around the Block. "The only time they really do a job is when dopers come around."	Only two participants detect a negative change in style when comparing their present and past communities, i.e., slow response time.	To raise children who respect others. Only one participant voiced a role in aiding officers. Fear of retribution.
Female Adults II	Participants know only two of current EAI staff.	Centered around the block and drug patrol.	Detect a difference where "it's actually worse" due to response time and service delivery with multiple police units within area.	Expressed a role in aiding officers but expressed a fear of retribution due to lack of anonymity.

(continued on next page)

TABLE 4.3
(continued)

Groups	Knowing Community Residents	Role as EAI Officer	Policing Style	Residents' Role
EAI Cops	Lack of personal knowledge of majority of community residents.	To get back in touch with community, to help others.	Can detect a difference where new style encourages officers to interact with community.	To provide information on drug dealers and other criminals.
EAIEP	Lack of personal knowledge of majority of community residents.	To get back in touch with community & to network.	New style encouraged interaction between officers and residents & is associated with conflict.	To work with police officers in solving community problems.
EAISCH	Personal knowledge of limited residents.	To equitably deliver services and to foster cooperation and involvement.	New style encourages cooperation and involvement of residents.	To become active in combatting community problems by working with police.

tance of citizen interaction (Trojanowicz & Bucqueroux, 1990; 1994; Trojanowicz & Moore, 1988; Trojanowicz, 1992; Vernon & Lasley, 1992; Miller & Hess, 1994). Focus-group participants, however, conceded having contact with housing police officers and zone officers, especially as these officers responded to citizen complaints and calls. Limited knowledge of some EAI officers was expressed by one member of the Female Children's group and by all members of the Female Adults II group. Members of the Female Adults II group acknowledged knowing two of the seven EAI officers. The member in the Female Children's group acknowledged knowing a "couple" of them, but couldn't recall their names. Additionally, members of the Teenage Male Juvenile Offenders group admitted having limited contact with, and knowledge of, some EAI officers.

All residents were aware of the new policing structure and were somewhat familiar with the roles of community policing officers in the East Athens community. Many groups, unsuspectingly yet accurately, described the role of EAI officers as just "hanging around the block" and curtailing and/or dismantling the drug trade within the community.

Generally, the majority of participants did not emphasize being mutual partners with patrolling officers in combatting and solving community problems. This contrasts with the research on the role and importance of community residents in developing and sustaining effective community-oriented policing endeavors (Miller & Hess, 1994; Sloan et al., 1992; Sill, 1991). Citizen groups generally described their role in the community as one of raising children to respect others and their property, building a rapport with the younger generation, looking out for one another, staying out of trouble, and advising friends to stay out of trouble. In contrast, participants in the Teenage Male Juvenile Offenders' group did not see themselves as having a role in the community. They expressed more laissez-faire attitudes and simply exhorted community residents to mind their own business. This sentiment was echoed by the all members of the Male Children's group, except one, the son of a deputy sheriff.

The vast majority of participants within all groups did not mention the need to aid officers in solving crimes or to provide information to police. In the process, they seemed to ignore the roles residents must play in community policing. However, some participants did appreciate the need for community residents to aid police officers in solving the problems of the community. One member of the Female Children group agreed that there is a need for community involvement, but did not know of or understand the role that community residents have in the concept of community policing.

> All of us should play a role in keeping the community safe. 'Cause like the police, they can't do it all by themselves and . . . I just can't think of what the role is that we should play in helping to keep the community safe.

Participants in the Female Adults II group also recognized the need for aiding officers in solving community problems.

> If you live in this community, you have to watch out for this community. You have to help your community along with yourself. . . . I play my role in calling the police instead of closing my eyes.

These opinions were shared by members of the Elderly group, as well as one participant within the Female Adult I group.

In general, all participants in the Male Children group, with the exception of the son of a deputy sheriff, expressed a no interest in helping officers solve community problems.

> I wouldn't help them if somebody paid me $10,000. . . . Me neither. I wouldn't take it.

However, one participant, the same son of a deputy sheriff, stated that he would help, but only in a "movie" or fictional situation. The group greeted his assertion with derision.

Residential focus-group participants unanimously agreed

that fear is a major obstacle in aiding officers in solving community problems. The greatest fear participants raised was the fear of retribution.

> You may wake up, if you got a car, and all your tires be slashed. You just hate to say something. . . . I ain't about to be killed over somebody else. . . . I may know what happened, but I ain't giving away no names. . . . If you stop somebody from doing something, you better carry something. . . .

> There is a girlfriend of mine that works on the police force and she comes to my house and be calling me out to her car. I told her, "I don't need no harm. If you can't come in plain clothes and talk to me like you been doing, then don't come to my house in no police car talking to me."

Another important concern was the lack of anonymity.

> When I see drugs, I tell it. Without that tip hotline I wouldn't do it because the police will come and tell them what you said. . . .

> I have a problem with calling the police because when you call the 911 number, they want to know your name and address. Then, when the police come to the place where you ask them to come, they give your name. . . . See that's the problem, and my car getting shot up.

Fear of retribution seemed to differ from the general fear of random, indiscriminate crime that is prevalent in the community and highlighted in the community policing literature (Moore, 1992, Trojanowicz & Bucqueroux, 1990; 1994; Skolnick & Bayley, 1986; Miller & Hess, 1994). However, focus-group participants also feared retribution or planned, non-random retaliation aimed at specific individuals as a result of their cooperation with police officers. Grinc's 1994 research on problems in stimulating community involvement in community policing called attention to this obstacle.

EAI officers expressed knowing some community residents, but only a limited number, primarily because of minimal contact and involvement of residents. Officers unanimously agreed that officers had to increase their interaction with community residents, as well as community residents increasing their interaction and cooperation with officers.

> One thing that I see we need to do and we hadn't really done it, but we need to pretty much stay on top of it, is going door to door and talking more with the citizens in the community. . . . We have to get back in touch with the people.

Similarly, officers suggested developing some kind of interaction or team building with community residents, inclusive of all age groups.

All officers were cognizant of their duties as a community policing officer, as well as the philosophy of community policing. In general, they tended to describe their role within the community policing structure as one of getting back to the basics of networking and interacting with residents.

> Just getting back to the basics . . . Like taking a big town and taking a small town mentality . . . Officer now networks and knows the people in his community and they know him . . . get in with the community and gain their trust and let them know that they can, if they have a problem, come and talk to you about it . . . I talk with the children. Sometimes I play with the children. Go play basketball over at the community center.

All of this was well illustrated in "one-on-one" interviews with one officer who expressed his role as a community policing officer as twofold: to be fair and to foster citizen cooperation.

> My job is to make sure that services are delivered fairly to everybody. . . . If I am going to provide a service to

calls to residents in Five Points, then I think the people of East Athens deserve the same consideration for a call no matter what.

These and other officer viewpoints are consistent with research on the roles of the police in effective community-oriented policing endeavors (Trojanowicz & Bucqueroux, 1994; Miller & Hess, 1994). Scholars highlight the importance of police-community bridge or coalition building, and the equitable treatment and delivery of police and other public services.

Relatedly, all officers were aware of the role that residents of the community must play in community policing. The officers generally agreed that citizen involvement and cooperation were minimal and unsatisfactory. They emphasized the need for more cooperation and involvement of community residents as viable partners in the community oriented policing structure of East Athens.

We need cooperation from everybody, from all status . . . it is going to take total cooperation to make East Athens totally safe . . . cooperation from both the police and the community because it is going to take both, the community and the police, working together. Because there is no way the public can solve it by themselves and there is no way that we can solve it by ourselves.

Empowerment

A set of questions was put to focus-group participants to assess their level of empowerment or sociopolitical activity. Specifically, community residents were asked to identify whether or not they engage in any individual or group activities that seek to improve their community, to identify if they had suggested any improvements to officers or community leaders, and to identify what community improvements were needed. Likewise, officers were asked to identify any groups or individuals who seek to improve the East Athens community and what improvements, if any, have been suggested to them. They were also asked if they had suggested any improvements to community residents or the local police and/or governmental administration, and if they had offered their personal community improvement suggestions. The general responses of all focus groups are summarized in Table 4.4 and examined in the ensuing paragraphs.

Community focus-group members generally participated in community-oriented or community-sponsored groups and activities (i.e., East Athens Community Center, Boys' and Girls' Club, Nellie B Tenant's Association, local churches, etc.). Only one member (in the Female Adults II group), out of all community focus groups, acknowledged being involved with an organization outside of the community, specifically the National Organization of Women (NOW). As noted in chapter 3, these participants were atypical of general residents in the East Athens community. Generally, residents seemed disengaged and were not open to participate in focus group discussions. So, one could infer that those participating might be least critical and the most active.

Within the residential focus groups, there was little direct participation with the East Athens Initiative staff, community leaders, and other local service providers. This lack of direct involvement, or the disinclination to suggest improvements to the appropriate channels, seemed to correlate directly with the fears outlined earlier, especially retribution, and lack of anonymity. This clearly contrasts with research on the attributes of successful community-oriented policing, that is, the reduction in communal fear of crime (Miller & Hess, 1994; Trojanowicz & Bucqueroux, 1994; 1990; Skolnick & Bayley, 1986; Sparrow et al., 1990). The prevalence of the communal fear of retribution, which inhibited community cooperation and involvement, parallels the findings of Grinc (1994) and Weatheritt (1983, 1987). Additionally, members of the Teenage Male Juvenile Offenders group indicated they were not comfortable approaching or even suggesting things to officers, largely because of a fear of continual harassment (e.g., "If you do

TABLE 4.4
EMPOWERMENT: SOCIOPOLITICAL ACTIVITY

Groups	Group or Individual Activities	Suggestions to Officers or Community Leaders	Community Improvement Suggestions
Teenage Male I	Boy's Club, Project RAP, Enlight Program.	No suggestions considered.	Drug- and violence-free places, more police presence, more interaction between officers and residents.
Teenage Male II	All attend East Athens Community Center.	No suggestions considered. ("They ain't got time for what you say.")	Respect from cops, quicker response time, use volunteers and video cameras to combat drug trade.
Teenage Female	All attend East Athens Community Center.	No suggestions considered.	Quicker response time, more officers on patrol, for officers to become acquainted with citizens, officers to live in community and "show people they care."
Teenage Male Juvenile Offenders	No participation in group or individual activities.	No suggested improvements. Fear of harassment by officers.	Role models, structured activities for teens, quicker response time, no officer harassment.
Female Children	All attend East Athens Community Center.	No suggested improvements, except for one participant.	More officers, officers to reside in community, "more caring police," integrated police units.

(continued on next page)

TABLE 4.4
(continued)

Groups	Group or Individual Activities	Suggestions to Officers or Community Leaders	Community Improvement Suggestions
Male Children	All attend East Athens Community Center. Neighborhood trash pick-up.	No suggested improvements.	More respect from officers, no officer harassment, to dismantle drug trade.
Elderly	All attend neighborhood church.	Suggestions have been made privately. Fear of retribution.	For officers "to do the same thing they been doing."
Female Adults I	Active members of Nellie B's Tenant Association.	Two participants have suggested improvements, but a fear of association is apparent in group.	More foot patrols, quicker response time, responsible parents, need for EAI cops to spend more time away from the Block area, respect from officers, more interaction from officers.
Female Adults II	Active members of Nellie B's Tenant Association. One participant is a member of National Organization of Women.	Participants have suggested improvement via letters and community forums.	Quicker response time, responsible parents, for police to be more involved with community, respect from officers, officers to respect anonymity of citizens, community parenting, enforcement of curfew laws, and neighborhood fencing and lighting.

(continued on next page)

TABLE 4.4
(continued)

Focus Groups	Group or Individual Activities	Suggested Improvements	Community Improvement Suggestions
EAICOPS	Nellie B's Tenant Association, St. Mark AME Church, Rev. Killian, and "business owners."	Only one suggestion (from a business owner).	More support and involvement from community, increased support from police and local administration, structured activities for juveniles, support from judicial system, positive role models, state and federal aid.
EAIEP	"Muslims," St. Mark AME Church, Nellie B's Tenant Association, and other citizen groups.	Parents suggest safe surroundings for kids, reducing drugs and criminal activity.	More support and involvement from residents, local, state, and federal governments, University community, more structured activities, legitimate businesses, more interaction.
EAISCH	Nellie B Tenants Association, East Athens Human Resources Committee.	Nellie B Tenant's suggested curfew enforcement.	More involvement from residents, community comradery, reformation of juvenile justice system, and a proactive local government.

that [then] they will sweat you more."). The Teenage Males II group added that officers really do not care to listen to what teenagers have to say, unless it is a major case and a reward being offered.

Members of the two Female Adult groups were active in suggesting improvements to the EAI staff and local authorities. Many, via the Nellie B Tenants' Association, indicated they have suggested improvements to the police and other authorities, suggestions directly related to enforcing laws (e.g., loitering, public drunkenness, teenage curfew, etc.), quicker response times, officers' involvement and/or visibility in the community, and physical improvements (e.g., fencing and lighting around areas of drug infestation). However, they stated that the response of the local authorities was generally negative (e.g., budget restraints).

In most groups, three major community improvement suggestions were consistently aired by residents: quicker response time; an increase in the number of officers and an extension of the East Athens Initiative to the more general East Athens community; and better treatment by or respect from community officers. However, some suggestions seemed to converge or cluster around age groups.

The Teenage Males I group and Teenage Male Juvenile Offenders both suggested a need for positive role models in the community, as well as the need for more drug and violence-free places for youth activities. Additionally, the Teenage Males I group and the group of Teenage Females stated that officers needed to build a rapport with the community by becoming more involved and active. The Female Children group and the group of Teenage Females suggested that officers ought to live in some of the vacant public housing apartments or houses within the community. Both groups thought that this would deter illegal activity in the area. The two Female Adult groups emphasized the need for parents to accept their child-rearing responsibilities. Furthermore, both groups repeated requests for officers to serve, protect, and respect all citizens regardless of their economic situations.

To treat us the same way as they treat people out in Forest heights, Kingswood, Five Points, University Heights . . . They think that because we don't live in houses and stuff that we are lower than a man.

In some contrast, the Elderly focus group expressed a general satisfaction with the current state of the community. Their sentiments highlighted clear generational differences in satisfaction when compared to other citizen groups. Members of this group recounted the foregone days when officers did not serve, or take into account any of the neighborhoods of East Athens. Therefore, members expressed satisfaction with the services that the local government and police officers now provide, and concluded that officers needed to continue to do the same things that they have been doing.

East Athens Initiative officers identified two religious organizations (Muslims and St. Mark AME Church), the local public housing tenants' association, the East Athens Human Resources Committee, and community business owners as groups and individuals seeking to improve the Nellie B area. However, officers voiced concern over the limited number and scope of suggested improvements offered by these groups and individual residents.

Their main concern is their children. "Are my children going to be safe? I want a safe place for my children. I don't want my child to be in a bad environment."

These same officers reported that residents demanded certain services, but did not seem to recognize the reciprocal relationship associated with community policing.

We don't want crime! We don't want drugs! We don't want this! They say that but yet, we don't get a phone call from someone when the drug dealers are on the corner selling dope.

Interestingly similar to community residents, police officers did not suggest improvements to residents, or to officials of the police or local governmental administration. Their general prescriptions for community improvement tended to fall into three categories: (1) more support and involvement from residents of Nellie B and East Athens; (2) more support from the local police administration; and (3) more support from the university community, as well as the local, state, and federal government.

> I think the involvement is there but there's certain people that are always involved and there's certain people that just don't care. . . . We would like to see everybody get involved. . . . I think the level of involvement is not nearly enough, especially for East Athens. . . . We need cooperation from everybody. From all status.

> I think we need some more backing, especially from the administration of the department. Half of them don't even know where the block [is] at. They don't know the substation. I have never seen our chief in this area before. . . . Stop talking the talk and lets walk the walk. We are working with just hand me down things. As far as our vehicles over here, we get what is left. We have the smallest amount of equipment to do the job, the smallest amount of resources in the police department.

Officers emphasized the need for increased funding and support by the local government, especially to build community parks and recreation facilities. Similarly, they argued for increased state and federal funds to install air conditioners and/or ceiling fans in apartments. By improving living conditions, the officers argued, the likelihood of kids being out of the home during the hot summer nights would decrease. In contrast to the majority of officers and in a one-on-one interview, one officer voiced satisfaction with the support of the local police administration.

> I am fairly satisfied with the administration because since the inception of the East Athens Initiative, we got

our own little radio system. . . . We've got two bicycles that should be here any day now. . . . I'm getting two new police cars as soon as they get them ready.

Other suggestions raised by individual officers included the need for positive role models for children, the need of legitimate businesses in the community, and the reformation of the judicial system, including juvenile justice.

SUMMARY

In this chapter the general responses of focus groups to four major issues were set out. A summary chart highlights these responses and is found in Table 4.5. In general, all groups, both citizens and officers, saw drugs and related problems as the major community problem of East Athens. Additionally, citizens expressed considerable dissatisfaction with police service delivery. This resonated in all groups with the sole exception of the Elderly. Community officers called attention to an incremental, torpid, yet positive, change in citizen satisfaction with police services in the move to community-oriented policing.

Knowledge of the ideals and philosophy of community policing was absent in most citizen groups, but clearly pronounced with the local police officers. Lack of community and individual involvement, as well as general ignorance of individual and communal roles in community policing, were apparent across groups. Underlying this lack of both association and public involvement was a real fear of retribution. East Athens residents were clearly afraid to cooperate with local police in any jurisdiction. This lack of community involvement was also emphasized by police officers who called for increased interaction between officers and residents.

The level of community empowerment, identified as sociopolitical activity and expressed in terms of suggestions for community improvement, was also low in the citizen focus groups. Officers also recognized this. Again, fear of ret-

TABLE 4.5
DESCRIPTIVE PROFILE OF FOCUS GROUPS

Groups	Problems	Satisfaction	Enlightenment	Empowerment
Teen Males I	Violence and drugs	"So-so" (i.e., slow response time)	Lack of direct knowledge of EAI officers; no role in aiding police	Lack of direct input to EAI staff
Teen Males II	Drugs and violence	Dissatisfied because cops are not "really doing nothing" and slow response time	Lack of direct knowledge or involvement with EAI; fear of having a role	Lack of direct input b/c "they ain't gonna listen"
Teen Female	Drugs, violence, and shootings	Dissatisfaction based on slow response time	Lack of knowing EAI officers; no involvement based on fear of retribution	Lack of direct input to EAI staff
TMJO	Drugs, violence, lack of role models	Dissatisfaction based on slow response time; hate and contempt toward cops	Limited knowledge of EAI cops; no role in aiding EAI cops	Lack of direct input to EAI or other cops

(continued on next page)

TABLE 4.5
(continued)

Groups	Problems	Satisfaction	Enlightenment	Empowerment
Female Children	Teens involved with drugs and violence	Dissatisfaction because of perception of cops not caring for community	Lack of direct knowledge of EAI cops; role was expressed by one subject	Lack of direct input to EAI staff
Male Children	Police, drug dealers, violence	Dissatisfaction based on negative experiences	Lack of direct knowledge of cops and interest in aiding cops	Lack of direct input to EAI staff
Elderly	Drugs and related activities	Very high based on reflecting on the present and past	Lack of direct knowledge of EAI staff; expressed a fear in too active of a role	All are active but are apprehensive
Female Adults I	Drugs, violence, alcohol, violent music, and loitering	Dissatisfaction because of slow response, lack of respect for residents, and policing structure	Lack of direct knowledge of EAI staff; lack of role in aiding cops b/c of fear of getting involved	Some have been active in suggesting improvements; fear of retribution

(continued on next page)

(continued on next page)

TABLE 4.5
(continued)

Groups	Problems	Satisfaction	Enlightenment	Empowerment
Female Adults II	Drugs, teen pregnancy, domestic abuse, killings, lack of parental responsibility	Dissatisfaction because of policing structure, slow response time, and negative experiences; satisfaction with initial experiences with new East Athens Sergeant	Direct knowledge of two East Athens officers; knowledgeable about their role in solving community problems	Have suggested improvements to East Athens officers and other authorities
EAICOPS	Drugs and its related behavior	Satisfaction on the increase (past-present experiences)	Knowledgeable about some residents but expressed a need for more interaction	Recognized some groups that lend support to EAI staff and East Athens Community

TABLE 4.5
(continued)

Groups	Problems	Satisfaction	Enlightenment	Empowerment
EAIEP	Drug and alcohol abuse, high crime; lack of community involvement	Satisfaction on the increase due to switch to community policing	A need for officers to interact with community residents; also expressed a need for residents to interact with officers	Recognized some groups and individuals that are supportive of EAI; a need for more involvement and support
EAISCH	Drugs, lack of community involvement and cooperation, a need to build rapport with kids	Satisfaction on the increase but slowly changing based on past and present experiences of residents; satisfaction on increase based on community involvement	Direct contact and involvement with only certain residents by EAI staff, minimal level of community involvement and cooperation	Recognized some groups are supportive; a need for more community support in taking control of their neighborhood

ribution was described by citizens as an underlying reason.

Several themes emerged in these focus-group discussions, of which five seem most important. These include: (1) negative experiences of participants or significant others with police; (2) lack of personal or individual knowledge of residents on the part of EAI officers; (3) lack of respect for the East Athens community residents by police officers; (4) disparate service delivery; and (5) lack of citizen participation and/or support based on fear of retribution. Two major themes surfaced in officer focus group discussions. These include a need for more support from the community, local, state, and federal governments, and an expansion of community-oriented policing initiative within East Athens and Clarke County in general. More sustained analysis of these themes will be provided in chapter 5.

CHAPTER 5

AN ANALYSIS OF CITIZEN THEMES

Even though focus-group interviewing is not designed to reach consensus but to examine perceptions, attitudes, and opinions on a given topic of discussion (Morgan, 1988), little variation in opinions, attitudes, and perceptions emerged from the citizen discussion groups. Two areas of consensus were evident in the analysis of citizen focus-group discussions: fear of crime or retribution and negative perspectives on law enforcement. These findings have particular relevance because of the nonrepresentative character of focus-group interviewing and the potential establishment of a "group think" phenomenon (Lederman, 1989).

A real fear of retribution was evident in each focus group. Regardless of the age and gender of participants, fear of retribution was emphasized in all focus groups. The limited range of citizens' perspectives is unusual, yet with confidence the researcher has concluded that the consensus of opinions was not a function of group think, but the function of a real and ever-present fear of crime that surpassed both age and gender barriers. There was also considerable consensus about the quality of police service delivery. With some exceptions, most participants were not positive, although this criticism was not as pronounced as the aforementioned fear of retribution. As noted in chapter 4, the Elderly seemed more satisfied with police service delivery in general and community policing in particular. This general dissatisfaction is particularly noteworthy when one recognizes the nonrepresentative character of the sample. If these participants, who were willing to participate and who were assumed to be more positive in their general outlook, were this negative, what must be the general opinion and perceptions in the community?

Five major themes echoed throughout the focus group discussions of East Athens residents. These themes typically cut across all gender and age group lines. They include: (1) negative perceptions of police interactions; (2) perceived lack of personal or individual knowledge of EAI officers by residents; (3) perceived lack of respect by police officers toward the East Athens community and its residents; (4) perceived disparate service delivery to the East Athens community; and (5) general passivity or apathy on the part of East Athens residents.

In this chapter, these themes will be analyzed against the findings of previous research on urban service delivery, citizen satisfaction, and community policing. Specifically, this chapter will compare and contrast the findings of this study with previous research by focusing on two major questions: Do the relevant literatures yield similar themes and paint similar pictures? and what explanations are advanced by the literature and are they applicable in these instances?

NEGATIVE INTERACTIONS WITH POLICE

Since the urban unrest and turbulence of the 1960s, many have studied citizen perceptions and attitudes toward the police. Additionally, many have examined black-and-white perceptions of police and other urban services (Hahn, 1971; Aberbach and Walker, 1970; Schuman and Gruenberg, 1968; Fogelson, 1968; U.S. President's Commission on Law Enforcement and Administration of Justice, 1967). Citizen surveys have increasingly been incorporated in the evaluations of police strategies. In this and other research, it is clear that police-citizen contacts have a direct impact on the perceptions of police by individuals (Lasley et al., 1995; Cordner and Jones, 1995; Cooper, 1980; Jefferson, 1991).

These studies have examined how citizen assessments of their contacts with the police influence their more general attitudes toward the police, as well as how general attitudes influence the assessment of individual contact (Brandl et al., 1994; Easton, 1965). In this research, questions remain on whether specific interactions affect general attitudes or if pre-existing, general attitudes affect specific assessments (Brandl et al., 1994). This query is captured in the work of Koenig:

> It is debatable whether perceived police rudeness and unfairness [in a specific incident] lead to less favorable public evaluations of local police, or whether less favorable evaluations of local police lead to the perception of neutral behaviors as incidents of rudeness or unfairness. (1980:248)

An issue related to this "chicken-egg" dilemma concerns attitudinal change. Specifically, how can existing negative attitudes toward the police be unfrozen and more positive attitudes strengthened? Lasley, Vernon, and Dery (1995) examined the different forms of police-citizen contact, the frequency of contact, the locations of contact, and the quality of contact to determine which type of contact affected the most pronounced change in citizen attitudes and which was most instrumental in building police-citizen partnerships. They (1995) concluded that residents who claimed to have made at least one physical contact with Operation Cul-De-Sac (OCDS) officers evidenced a 38 percent improvement in attitudes toward police-community partnerships, compared to a 12 percent improvement with residents who claimed that their only contact was of a visual nature. Additionally, they noted

> The frequency impact of physical contact between citizen and police was nearly two times higher than that observed for contact that was visual only. Specifically,

residents who made a daily personal contact with officers improved their relationship with police by a margin
of 69 percent [compared to 33%]. By comparison, a
weekly contact resulted in a 32 percent improvement
[compared to 14%], and a 19 percent improvement [com-
pared to 9%] was the result of making contact only once
per month. (1995:61)

Among those making personal contact with police, contact
in the home improved partnership attitudes to a much larger
extent (29%) than did contact made in the streets (17%).
However, those citizens who made contact with police in
both their homes and in the streets improved their attitudes
by 34 percent (1995:61).

In terms of quality of contact, Lasley et al. (1995) found
that when officers seemed to "care about residents as a person" there was pronounced improvement in citizen satisfactions and opinions of the community-police partnership.
Similarly, when officers took the time to understand the particulars of a problem, there were significant improvements in
citizens' opinions.

The results of this study offer some contrast to those of
Lasley et al. (1995). Specifically, negative interactions, contacts, or experiences that participants, their family members,
or friends had with the police emerged as a key factor in citizen focus-group discussions. These negative experiences left
a "nasty" taste in the mouths of participants and seemed, in
many instances, to constitute the essence of their dissatisfaction and disaffection with local police service delivery and
community policing.

As noted previously, East Athens residents reported a
lack of knowledge of, and infrequent, if any, personal contact
with, community policing officers. The police-citizen contacts that did take place occurred primarily in the streets and,
in general, carried negative connotations (i.e., traffic stop,
questioning, etc.). These contacts were perceived by residents
as "officer harassment," were reported as unwarranted stops,
and reinforced the negative interactions mentioned above.

Additionally, East Athens residents did not express the same type or quality of police-citizen contacts that Lasley et al. (1995) noted. In contrast to the politeness, helpfulness, caring, and understanding of LAPD's Operation Cul-De-Sac community policing officers, East Athens residents thought the community police officers were generally insensitive to community needs.

Citizen focus group discussions frequently underscored the pervasiveness of all of these negative interactions with police. With the exception of the Elderly, this theme resounded in all groups and generally transcended both gender and age. Furthermore, the negative interactions, contacts, and experiences seemed to be the most important determinant of citizen attitudes toward the police. This reinforces Scaglion and Condon's contention that "personal contact with police is a more significant variable" than the combined variables of race, gender, age, or socioeconomic status" (1980:490).

LACK OF KNOWLEDGE

Community policing, in essence, is an example of "group coproduction" where producer and consumer spheres overlap.

> Group coproduction involves voluntary, active participation by a number of citizens and may require formal coordination mechanisms between service agents and citizen groups. Perhaps the best example of group coproduction is the neighborhood watch group or neighborhood association where individuals join together in an effort to improve the quantity and/or quality of services consumed. (Brudney and England, 1983:63)

This type of coproduction consists of an active, participative, cooperative, and collective citizenry which seeks to enhance the quality of services that are delivered (Brudney and England, 1983). Whitaker describes this type of coproduction as "citizen/agent mutual adjustment" where citizens and agents interact in order to become sensitive to each other's service expectations and actions.

> In some public service delivery situations, agents and citizens interact to establish a common understanding of the citizen's problem and what each of them can do to help deal with it. This reciprocal modification of expectations and actions involves more communication than a simple request for assistance. (1980: 244)

Previous research on implementing, developing, and sustaining effective community policing has emphasized the need for opening and maintaining dual lines of communication between the community and the police (Trojanowicz, 1992; Trojanowicz, 1994; Trojanowicz & Moore, 1988). Furthermore, that research highlights the need for community officers to engage actively in interactions with community residents in order to identify the needs and concerns of their respective communities (Brown, 1989; Metchik & Winton, 1995). All of this requires a critical mix or bilateral alliance in coproducing such services (Whitaker, 1980; Brudney & England, 1983). Ideally, this will foster a sense of comraderie by helping to diminish community anxiety and animosity.

Previous research on determinants of attitudes toward police identified police-citizen personal contacts and interactions as important variables in this process (Decker, 1981; Lasley et al., 1995). As noted earlier, Scaglion and Condon emphasized that "personal contact with police is a more significant variable" than the combined variables of race, gender, age, and socioeconomic status (1980:490). In contrast to these prescriptions, there was a clear lack of individual/personal contact or even familiarity between the East Athens Initiative officers and the citizens included in the focus groups. All participants indicated that they had limited, if any, personal contact or individual knowledge of community policing officers who worked in their community. The limited amount of individual contact and knowledge was also conceded in the Elderly focus group, the one most supportive of and satisfied with the East Athens Initiative community policing venture. This clearly contrasts with the basic premise of community policing, that is, increasing personal contact with residents in hopes of building positive police-community interactions and establishing a successful, coproducing partnership (Trojanowicz & Bucqueroux, 1994; Trojanowicz & Moore, 1988; Brown, 1990; Brown, 1991).

In some instances, community residents' limited knowledge of EAI officers contrasted with the comparatively higher level of personal knowledge of, and in some instances greater respect for, public housing and zone/patrol police officers. Excluding the Elderly, residents could recognize only two EAI officers. Furthermore, participants indicated that they had little individual contact with those officers, as well as the remaining five officers of the East Athens Initiative unit. Some members of both Female Adult groups were familiar with specific housing police officers, but had very limited knowledge of or contact with East Athens community policing officers. As noted earlier, this limited contact contravenes one of the most important dimensions of community policing, that is, increased positive and personal officer-citizen contact.

These general findings parallel the research of Lasley and Vernon (1992) and Lasley et al. (1995) who studied the community policing effectiveness of LAPD's Operation Cul-De-Sac in changing community perceptions, raising community awareness, and cultivating police-citizen partnerships within inner-city communities. Lasley et al. noted the negative impact of infrequent, nonpersonal police-citizen contacts, and highlighted the tremendous impact of personal, frequent, positive, police-citizen interactions.

> Community-based policing can be used as an effective tool to "unfreeze" perceptual gaps between police and citizens. As discovered here, this appears to be the case even in inner-city neighborhoods where crime, lack of community presence, and deep-rooted anxieties toward police are typically found. (1995:61)

Moreover, these findings all add credence to the significance of "personal contacts" as espoused by Scaglion and Condon (1980).

Successful community policing requires that residents recognize and be familiar with specific officers. In Kratcoski et al.'s Cleveland study, citizens were more familiar with the community policing officers than the district or zone patrol officers who worked in their communities. Moreover, they expressed greater satisfaction with community policing mini-station officers than district officers. All of this led the authors conclude that

> No doubt much of the positive sentiment toward the mini-station police developed as a result of the citizens participation in Crime Watch Programs. (1995:208)

> The very presence of the mini-station officers in the neighborhood and their activity in a neighborhood Crime Watch Program is a major factor affecting the attitudes of citizens toward the police and their satisfaction with the police. (1995:210)

As highlighted in chapter 4, the lack of individual or personal knowledge was more pronounced in the Teenage and Children's focus groups. With the exception of the deputy sheriff's son, all participants in the Teenage Male Juvenile Offenders and Male Children focus groups and one member of the Teenage Female group seemed reluctant to establish any rapport with community policing officers. The focus group discussions, then, showed little, if any, of the attributes of community policing. These findings parallel the research on the limited impact of community policing on inner city, African-American neighborhoods conducted by Grinc (1994), while they contrast with the positive impact of community policing on African-Americans highlighted in the research of Kratcoski et al. (1995), Lasley et al. (1995), Lasley and Vernon (1994), Trojanowicz (1982), and Trojanowicz and Banas (1985). Specifically, fear of retribution was still present, a general lack of individual or personal knowledge of community policing officers still existed, and consequently, a working partnership between the community and officers was not evident. These findings highlight the very limited implementation of community policing within the East Athens community.

Perhaps contributing to the seemingly limited impact of community policing, or perhaps reflective of it, was the limited knowledge of the ideals or philosophy of community policing that emerged in all focus-group discussions. When asked specifically about the concept of community policing, few groups fully recognized or seemed to understand the notion of coproduction or partnership with the officers of the East Athens Initiative. Neither did these citizen groups understand fully their respective roles. Ironically, only the Teenage Males I group seemed to appreciate the relevance of coproduction. This represents a departure from the process advocated by Trojanowicz (1992) Trojanowicz and Bucqueroux (1994), Trojanowicz and Moore (1988), Brown (1990), Brown (1991), and Sill (1991), all of whom emphasized the need to build a community-police partnership by initiating, maintaining, and cultivating frequent and positive citizen-police contacts. Relatedly, this also parallels Grinc's recent (1994) emphasis on stimulating community involvement in community policing. Grinc noted that one major problem facing community policing was the failure of community residents to understand fully their role in this policing system. Citizens' lack of knowledge of the ideals and philosophy of community policing, as well as their roles in it, can be summed up in the words of one Female Children participant:

> All of us should play a role in keeping the community safe, 'cause like the police, they can't do it all by themselves and . . . I just can't think of what the role is that we should play.

All of this contrasts to the community policing literature that emphasizes the need for "start-up" training of community residents, a training that fosters community input and support to engage effectively in this working partnership with the police (Trojanowicz, 1992; Trojanowicz, 1994; Trojanowicz & Carter, 1988; Trojanowicz & Moore, 1988; Sill, 1991; Maddox, 1993). More generally, these findings run counter to the basic premise of Brudney and England's collective, active, and positive coproduction of services, "which envisions direct citizen involvement in the design and the delivery of city services with professional service agents" (1983:59).

LACK OF RESPECT

Lack of respect of the rights of certain citizens and communities on the part of police officers has been a dominant theme in the assessments of police services as applied to poor and disadvantaged citizens. Numerous studies have concluded that poor, disadvantaged, and often minority populations perceive a lack of respect by patrolling police officers and subsequently rate service quality far lower than whites (Fogelson, 1968; Hahn, 1971; Rossi & Berk, 1974; Aberbach & Walker, 1978; Rossi et al., 1974; Radelet, 1986). Rossi and Berk concluded,

In part, because the quality of services received by blacks is often considerably lower than whites (and perhaps their needs for such services are higher), blacks are possibly more sensitive to variations in those services from place to place. (1974:757)

In this study, lack of respect by police officers toward the East Athens community and its residents was the predominate theme that resounded in all focus-group discussions. This applied to all police officers and to community officers, that is, the East Athens Initiative and public housing officers.

Lack of community respect by East Athens Initiative and public housing officers surfaced in four complaints: slow response time, lack of timely intervention, alleged officer harassment, and the general perception that officers didn't care about the East Athens community or its residents.

"'Cause if they did," in the words of one resident, "they would be helping more." Numerous examples of these incidents are found in the preceding chapter and mirror the findings of Rossi et al. (1974) and other researchers who draw attention to African-American perceptions of lack of respect and dissatisfaction with police services (Frustenberg & Wellford, 1973; Bloch, 1974; Fogelson, 1968; Cooper, 1980; Hahn, 1974; Chambliss, 1994).

Rossi et al. (1974) examined the perceptions of blacks related to local government service delivery and performance in fifteen major cities. Included in urban service delivery were police practices. In this regard, the authors found substantial variation in police and other local governmental practices. However, they noted that in cities where police departments engage in potentially abrasive patrol tactics in poor areas, black residents had more pronounced levels of complaints about police service delivery. In particular, respondents called attention to lack of respect, slow response time, police brutality, and officer harassment.

Similarly, Fogelson (1968) examined the reasons for the resentment and eventual confrontation by African Americans toward police officers. In the process, he identified four reasons for resentment and eventual confrontation: police brutality, police harassment, the lack of adequate police protection of black neighborhoods, and citizen sense of powerlessness to protest and remedy their grievances. Like Rossi et al. (1974), Fogelson also found that intensive police patrol and African-American perceptions of police officer harassment were significantly correlated.

These findings mirror the works of Frustenberg and Wellford (1973), Bloch (1974), and Fogelson (1968). Frustenberg and Wellford's evaluation of police calls revealed that blacks are more critical of and dissatisfied with the police services they received when compared to whites, especially in terms of police response time. Other than response time, their study indicated that blacks and whites rate police services comparably, something that contrasts with the perceptions of participants in this study.

The findings on response time of Frustenberg and Well-ford specifically mirror the findings of Bloch (1974) and contrast with those reported here. Bloch's case study of the distribution of police services in the affluent and poor communities of Washington, D.C., concluded that there was a high level of citizen satisfaction with police services, even in poor areas. However, Bloch noted that citizen surveys showed that in respect to response time, citizens in the poorer sections were dissatisfied with slower, unsatisfactory police response time. Fogelson (1968), like Frustenberg and Wellford and Bloch, also found a high level of dissatisfaction that bordered on resentment and festered into riots or confrontations. The correlation of slow response time and increased police resentment of these findings, mirror the perceptions and emotions of East Athens residents. This correlation has also been found in previous community policing research (Trojanowicz, Steele, & Trojanowicz, 1986).

This general perception that police officers did not care about residents in depressed, ghetto areas is repeated in the works of Fogelson (1968), Cooper (1980), and Hahn (1971) and mirrors the sentiments of the majority of community residents who participated in this study. For example, Hahn (1971) noted that 78 percent of respondent felt that officers were mainly interested in keeping the peace without trying to help solve community problems. Similarly, Fogelson (1968:233) noted that officers "ignore a wide range of illegal activities there, including drug addiction and prostitution, that they would not tolerate elsewhere." Given this evidence, Cooper noted that African Americans in ghetto areas "relate to a cop not as another human being as much as they relate to him as a thing which is distant and impassioned about the circumstances of the community in which he finds himself" (1980:139).

Similar to lack of respect for the community by community officers, lack of respect by police officers in general emerged from the analysis of focus group discussions. This seemed to have been fueled by incidents that occurred beyond the East Athens community. Several of these incidents were stated in various focus group discussions (Teenage Males I and Teenage Male Juvenile Offender groups) and presented in chapter 4.

> They caught me up town after somebody had robbed somebody. . . . They pulled all of us over and just checked me down. Then they grabbed me by the thumb and put the handcuffs on, set me in the back seat . . . So when they couldn't find nothing, they got mad. Then they tried to make like we had something. They took us up town and made us walk home. . . .

> I remember this night we were downtown. You remember that night we were downtown and them folks were shooting water and stuff at us? Oh, yeah, and the police didn't do nothing. Yeah, the police were right around the corner and they didn't do nothing. Yeah, they (cops) didn't even do nothing 'cause I think they were college students . . . they didn't do nothing.

This perception by participants contributed to a "blue suit generalization" phenomenon. This exists when residents negatively perceive and stereotype officers simply on the basis of their uniforms.

This phenomenon stemmed from the direct experiences of participants, as well as indirect or "hearsay" experiences of family members and friends. As a result, participants seemed to become more sensitive to the blue uniform of officers than the person. Relatedly, participants, particularly children and teenagers, tended to stereotype or generalize the police as "being bad," that is, an overly aggressive, noncaring, threatening force.

Other research supports this "blue suit generalization" phenomenon expressed by participants in East Athens (Jacob, 1971; Cooper, 1980; Wilson & Kelling, 1982). Particularly relevant is the work of Tony Jefferson. Jefferson's (1991) examination of British data on the attitudes, perceptions, and experiences of black people noted that those who have the most negative interactions with police, that is, young black males, are the most hostile and critical. Jefferson underscored that, as a consequence of these negative interactions, black youth were more likely to perceive the police as abusive, as using excessive force, and as fabricating evidence. These findings were repeated in the studies of Cashmore and McLaughlin (1991) who compared policing of black people in Britain and the United States.

Similarly, Herbert Jacob's study of "White and Black Perceptions of Justice" concluded that blacks perceive the police more negatively as a result of negative experiences where "they are severely threatened or sanctioned . . . thus the Negroes' less favorable evaluations of the actual policeman reported earlier is reflected in dissatisfaction with police services directly experienced or consumed" (1971:75–76). Likewise, Wilson and Kelling (1982) emphasized that minority communities and neighborhoods generate and reinforce negative attitudes due to "involuntary interactions with police" that are generally perceived as officer harassment. In some contrast, perhaps, to Wilson and Kelling, the participants in this study called attention to "involuntary interactions" beyond or outside the parameters of this community.

By comparing the findings of participants in this study to the findings of previous research, it is evident that there is empirical evidence to support the "blue suit generalization" phenomenon. Likewise, there is some consistency regarding explanatory factors. The negative incidents and involuntary interactions highlighted in this study are similar to those emphasized in the previous research (Jefferson, 1991; Cashmore & McLaughlin, 1991; Cooper, 1980; Wilson & Kelling, 1982) and tend to bolster both general and specific perceptions on the theme of respect.

The overall theme of lack of respect by officers was more pronounced within all male (i.e., Teenage, Juvenile Offenders, and Children) and both Female Adult groups. This also parallels previous research on African Americans that found younger males and women are more critical or dissatisfied with public services.

Several studies have suggested that younger respondents tend to be more critical of municipal services than older respondents (Williams, 1977; Wilbern & Williams, 1971; Stipak, 1974; Fitzgerald & Durant, 1980). Specifically, Thomas and Holmes (1992) analyzed the determinants of satisfaction for blacks and whites with data from the Quality of American Life Survey conducted in 1971 and replicated in 1978. Consistent with the findings from the previous research of Campbell et al. (1976) and Brown and Coulter (1983), they found a positive relationship between race, age, and gender that parallels the findings of this study.

Similarly, in Austin and Dodge's (1992) article, "Despair, Distrust, and Dissatisfaction Among Blacks and Women," race and gender were linked to discontent and dissatisfaction. In particular, the authors noted that black women expressed greater discontent and dissatisfaction when compared to all other gender and race groups, followed by black males.

Generally, males perceived officers as oppressive, with participants in the Male Children focus group explicitly describing them as nonliving, nonfeeling beings.

> I would describe them as selfish, coldhearted . . . I bet if I saw somebody in their family doing drugs I want to see if they would lock them up.

These perceptions mirror the findings of Cooper who states that ghetto residents

> relate to a cop not as another human being as much as they relate to him as a thing which is distant and impassioned about the circumstances of the community in which he finds himself . . . The ghetto residents do not see a person in a blue uniform, they see a minion of the establishment, the oppressor, a pig. (1980:138–139)

Cooper concludes that ghetto resident perceptions are the result of the lack of personal and positive interactions between residents and officers. These findings parallel the aforementioned research of Wilson and Kelling (1982), Jacob (1971), and Fogelson (1968).

Similarly, adult females also emphasized police lack of respect for community and individual rights and concluded that there was a disparate, socioeconomic or race-based, service delivery. Female Adults I group declared that officers

> look down on us because we stay in [public] housing. We are just the same as the people way over on the other side, at Five Points. We are just as good as them.

Additionally, members in this group expressed the need for officers

> to give respect. If a person calls you and you smell alcohol, that don't mean you disrespect them. . . . A little more respect to you when the police come to your house. If you call them, they think everything is your fault and then they think they shouldn't do nothing. You know they don't do nothing. They don't care about you. . . .

> Respect me as a person. . . . Give me the same respect that you would give a person out on Five Points. Give me that same respect. I don't care if I am black or white or green or yellow, give me respect. Talk to me as if I am a person, not something that you just don't want to have nothing to do with because I live in housing.

Members of the Female Adults II group expounded on these themes.

> All my neighbors are complaining of how they talk to the residents. How they treat them. The way they handle cases. They're not turning all those police reports in, because you turn a police report in, it goes down to the housing office, if you live in public housing. Some of the residents have complained that when they checked on it, there was no report at the office and it should be.

These perceptions by adult females mirror the afore-mentioned research of Austin and Dodge (1992), Jacob (1971), Cooper (1980), and Fogelson (1968). Furthermore, the under-lying factors parallel the Thomas and Holmes' point that black women exist in an environment that is both sexist and racist and often yields economic insecurity. These findings support the "double jeopardy" hypothesis advanced by Beale (1970) who argues that black adult females' dissatisfaction may be a result of the dynamics of economic insecurity brought on by the dual reality of racism and sexism. This has significant applicability to the participants in both Female Adult groups, as all but two were single mother heads of households.

Interestingly, one member of the Male Children group did not perceive a lack of respect by officers toward the East Athens community and its residents. Not coincidentally, this participant was the son of a female deputy sheriff. In contrast to other members of the Male Children focus group, this par-ticipant described officers as being "a little friendly, kind-hearted and they work to keep us safe." For this youngster, the impact of direct knowledge and frequent, positive, per-sonal interaction with his mother dispelled the view of offi-cers as being "a minion of the establishment, the oppressor, a pig."

The apparent impact of direct knowledge and frequent, positive, personal interaction adds credence to the sugges-tions of Cooper (1980) and Jefferson (1991). Cooper (1980) and Jefferson (1991) implied that more frequent, personal, and positive interactions between police and African Americans may decrease the male, ghetto youth's perception of officers as being "distant and impassioned" and may help to foster more positive perceptions of police officers and increase citi-zen satisfaction.

Another interesting gap was observed when comparing the Elderly's perception of lack of respect by police officers to participants within other citizen focus groups. As noted in chapter 4, participants within the Elderly focus group per-ceived community policing officers as being respectful and caring, not only for their welfare, but for the welfare of their community. This parallels findings in previous research that show a strong correlation between age and satisfaction (Thomas & Holmes, 1992; Brown & Coulter, 1983; Campbell et al., 1976) and contrasts to the perceptions of other citizen focus groups. Participants in the Elderly group in this study did not perceive a lack of respect for the community and its inhabitants by officers. In fact, this focus group expressed the opposite. These participants reflected on the times when police presence and protection were nonexistent within their community. Comparisons of past (both distant and not so distant) to present delivery of police and other governmental services seemed to explain these differences in satisfaction with police services and community policing. Interestingly, these citizens explicitly applauded the current efforts of the East Athens Initiative.

When I first moved over here, none of the streets were paved, didn't have no sewage, no water . . . it [police service and protection] used to be so bad with dope, where people couldn't sit out on the front porch . . . Right now at this time of day, only thing you could see was them smoking that stuff . . . only thing you could see right in them bushes was them lights coming on . . . would be sparkling out there where they would be lighting them pipes.

With some exceptions, residents generally emphasized a lack of respect by officers toward the East Athens community and its residents. These findings mirror the empirical evidence of previous research, albeit with some qualifications. Likewise, the explanations advanced by the literature are generally applicable in this instance. In turn, this theme of lack of respect draws one's attention to another issue, namely participants' concern with disparate service delivery.

DISPARATE SERVICE DELIVERY

Equitable service delivery by governmental entities has been and continues to be a point of contention for scholars of public administration and especially for municipal governments. Disparate service delivery has been an area of concern since the 1971 service equalization case, *Hawkins* v. *Town of Shaw* (437 F.2d 1286, 1287), which found the town of Shaw, Mississippi guilty of racial discrimination in the provision of various municipal services. Numerous studies have been conducted and have concluded that poor, disadvantaged, minority populations perceive disparate service delivery by local governments. Lineberry and Welch (1974) noted that service inequalities, real or imagined, may serve to intensify the poor's disaffection from local government. Similarly, the conclusions of the Kerner Commission found in its *Report of the National Advisory Commission on Civil Disorders* that

> Inadequate sanitation services are viewed by many ghetto residents not merely as instances of poor public service, but as manifestations of racial discrimination. This perception reinforces existing feelings of alienation and contributes to a heightened level of frustration and dissatisfaction, not only with the administrators of the sanitation department, but with all the representatives of local government. (1968:148)

In this study, a perception of disparate service delivery by the local police department toward residents of the Nellie B and Vine neighborhood of East Athens echoed throughout the various focus-group discussions. This pattern parallels two components of Lineberry's (1977) underclass hypothesis regarding the distribution of municipal services among urban neighborhoods. Lineberry postulated that "some groups suffer because of their race, because of their social status, or because of their paucity of political power" (1977:12).

Other studies have researched local government service delivery to explore, examine, and explain "Who Gets What?" and "Why?" (Lineberry & Welch, 1974; Lineberry, 1977; Lowry, 1968; Jones et al., 1978; Mladenka, 1980; Cingranelli, 1981; Bolotin & Cingranelli, 1983). Each emphasized, however, that it was difficult to obtain reliable data. For example, Lineberry and Welch (1974) noted three obstacles or problems to measuring the distribution of urban services. These include measuring service output in the context of intracity distributional research, choosing a standard in evaluating service patterns, and finding hard data on the distribution of public services. Therefore, it is hard to determine if perceptions of disparate service delivery are reality-based.

Regardless, residents in this study generally agreed that there was disparate service delivery. This was evident in their recollection of the treatment of two murder victims found in their neighborhood—a black female and a white male.

> You remember when that white man got killed up in Nellie B. It didn't take long for them to get that man out of there. . . . But a [black] lady had got killed down from where I stay at and she [her body] had stayed out there for most of the day . . . A long time . . . They had her just laying out there, she was butt-naked and everything, but she was dead. . . . It took a long time.

> Now he was in a car and they covered him up. A black girl got killed up on the block and they let her lay out there in the street for over an hour before they even put anything on her. . . . I can't understand why she would lay in the road like that and he was in a car and they covered him up before they even put him on the stretcher, and she didn't have on no clothes. . . .

> They told me that if they had covered up the body they could have took off some evidence. But you can not leave this woman's body sitting out like this. Kids are looking, adults, drunks, drug addicts, and everybody else is looking. . . . She was laying in ants . . . and the ants were just tearing her face all to pieces.

These dramatic incidents bolstered residents' perceptions of disparate service delivery. Additionally, they lent support to the aforementioned findings of Lineberry and

Welch (1974) and the Kerner Commission (1968). More important, these incidents reinforced existing feelings of alienation (i.e., being "second-class citizens").

> If the police treated us the same way as they treat people out in Forest Heights, Kingswood, Five Points, University Heights, and all that . . . They think that because we don't live in houses and stuff that we are lower than a man.

More compatible with the research findings reported here is research that suggests the rejection of Lineberry's underclass hypothesis might be premature. Cingranelli's (1981) study, which tested alternative models of municipal service distribution, found that black neighborhoods did not receive a smaller share of service benefits in the absolute sense. However, they did receive less than comparable white neighborhoods. Cingranelli argued that black neighborhoods have greater needs for urban services than others. Therefore, equal or near equal neighborhood-oriented services do not compensate in filling the "need gap." His study of Boston concluded that

> Black neighborhoods received higher per capita expenditures in an absolute sense, but they received lower expenditures per capita than comparable white neighborhoods—comparable especially in terms of political power and need for services. (1981:691)

Similarly, Bolotin and Cingranelli's (1983) analysis of equity and urban policy in the distribution of services, again using 1971 Boston data, suggested against a hasty rejection of the underclass hypothesis.

In almost all focus groups, residents emphasized three aspects of disparate service delivery: slow police response time, contemptuous treatment by police officers, and police organizational structure and subsequent confusion. As emphasized earlier, slow police response time was a key determinant of residents' disaffection toward the Athens-Clarke County Police Department and their perceptions of disparate service delivery. Slow response time was even more contentious with the establishment of a police "substation" within the East Athens community. When the police substation was established, residents expected better police response time. As noted in the preceding chapter, all focus groups, with the exception of the Elderly, were not satisfied and called for quicker police response time.

Many participants emphasized that slow response time was a result of socioeconomic-based service delivery, while the general quality of delivery of police services was based on the race of the service provider.

> Slow response . . . if you call the police and it takes them an hour to get here . . . if the police treated us the same way as they treat people out in Forest Heights, Kingswood, Five Points, University Heights and all that . . . They think that because we don't live in houses and stuff that we are lower than a man.

> I remember an incident where some men were out on the sidewalk shooting guns. I called nine-one-one and this white officer responded to the call. But when he got here, they had hid the guns. . . . He walks off and this black policeman comes up and looks around and the rifle was laying in front of this driveway. Therefore, the white officer was just nonchalant, but the black officer investigated. . . . I've told that sergeant, that they have up there, don't send no white officer to this neighborhood. They don't give a damn about us anyway.

Likewise, many participants expressed strong feelings of disparate service delivery, especially as they recalled major incidents or negative experiences where police response time was unsatisfactory in dealing even with life-and-death situations. Members of the Teenage Male Juvenile Offenders group in particular complained about disparate service delivery, especially as it related to reports of crime.

Now it took them an hour and they [robbers] done tied my cousin up and robbed him and they [police] ain't came yet . . . if that would have been something else, they would have hurried up and come over there . . . let it been a dope call or something . . . or somebody white neighborhood done got robbed.

By juxtaposing these perceptions of slow response time to the findings of Pate et al. (1976), a clearer picture emerges. Pate et al.'s analysis on the determinants and effects of police response time concluded:

Citizen expectations about response time was an intervening variable; the difference between citizen expectations and the response time they observed was the most significant predictor of their satisfaction with response time. . . . The best predictor of general attitudes toward the police was the citizens' level of satisfaction with the responding police officer. (1976:xiv)

The data presented here suggest that response time, when compared to other variables, may not be as crucial a determinant of citizen's evaluations of the police as has been hypothesized. It is possible that public assurances of rapid response may inadvertently result in citizen dissatisfaction, when response time exceed that which citizens have been led to expect (1976:xiv). Citizens' expectations of quicker response time were fueled by and even increased in the wake of the establishment of the police substation and the East Athens Initiative. The resulting frustration clearly illustrated that community residents were not fully aware of the organizational dynamics, arrangements, and complexity of the East Athens community policing initiative. Moreover, it was apparent that the police officials did not completely communicate the particulars of the initiative to residents. As a consequence, participants' lofty expectations tended to "inadvertently result in citizen dissatisfaction, when response time exceeds that which citizens have been led to expect" (Pate et al., 1976:xiv).

In general, the dissatisfaction with police response time expressed by the various focus groups parallels the aforementioned findings of Frustenberg and Wellford (1973), Rossi et al. (1974), Pate et al. (1976), and Bloch (1974). Specifically, more pronounced dissatisfaction by the female adults and the male teenage and children groups mirrors the aforementioned research of Jefferson (1991), Austin and Dodge (1992), and Brown and Coulter (1983), while the apparent generational gap coincides with the findings of Thomas and Holmes (1992), Jefferson (1991), Brown and Coulter (1983), Campbell et al. (1976).

Treatment by patrolling officers was another major component of residents' perceptions of race-based or socioeconomic-based service delivery. As stated in the preceding paragraphs and chapter, residents repeatedly complained of lack of respect, officer harassment, and unsatisfactory treatment by police officers toward the East Athens community and its citizens. These perceptions parallel the aforementioned findings of Cooper (1980), Fogelson (1968), Hahn (1971), Radelet (1986), and Carter (1983).

Police organizational structure was the final component of residents' perceptions of disparate service delivery. Within this East Athens community, three police units are employed: patrol or zone officers, public housing officers, and East Athens Initiative community policing officers. This organizational arrangement seemed to cause confusion, dissatisfaction, and disaffection on the part of community residents, especially in terms of which unit was to respond to calls. Furthermore, this organizational arrangement seemed at variance with the desires of most focus group participants who emphasized the need for the police to "get in touch with the community." This is instrumental in establishing effective community policing endeavors (Trojanowicz & Bucqueroux, 1990; 1994; Maddox, 1993; Brown, 1990; 1991) and can be compromised by overlapping jurisdictions.

Confusing organizational arrangements are potential detriments to community policing. Miller and Hess noted that "at the heart of most new approaches to policing is a return to the ancient idea of community responsibility for the welfare of society" (1994:16). Relatedly, the ideal of community policing rests on the premise that police and community residents work closely together to solve the problems of crime, physical and social disorder, and neighborhood decay (Trojanowicz & Bucqueroux, 1990; 1994). For example, Lee Brown (1990) stressed the importance of fostering understanding between the police and the citizens they are sworn to protect. Brown's (1989) analysis of Houston's community policing program noted that essential to gaining this understanding is the effectiveness of officers' communication skills. He emphasized that these skills require not only the ability to work cooperatively with residents and others to solve problems, but also the ability to listen. Brown, then, envisioned officers as being "a part of the community, not apart from it" (1989:6) and emphasized that

> Permanent interaction between officers and neighborhood residents and merchants is the first step toward identifying the community's problems. When the people of the community get involved and realize they have a voice in improving their quality of life, it creates good will and makes it easier for the police to fulfill their mission. (1991:6)

By contrasting these prescriptions to the expressions of focus-group participants, it becomes evident that gauging community sensitivity was neglected. Multiple and confusing organizational arrangements are not "user-friendly."

> Another problem with the police service is there are seven (7) officers assigned to public housing in all of Athens. If you get a call, you're only gonna get them. So if they are on Broad Street you'll have to wait. There's an [zone] officer sitting right over here, but if he's not assigned, he ain't coming. You're only gonna get an Athens housing officer.

I asked her, why did you bring the car back in the sub-station if they (EAI officers) can't work with housing authority also? . . . What was the point of bringing them back over here if they can't work in Nellie B too?

For this community to have just policemen for just this community and we call in for a policeman and the policemen that work in this community are not available, they tell us that they do not have any housing officers on duty. If they can work in other communities, why can't others come to this community and work? . . .

On their car it says "To Serve and Protect.". . . There shouldn't be no such thing as a housing police!! They should all be like you say, to serve and protect whoever the individual . . . If our policemen, as they put it, can go there, why not they come here when we need them?

It should be noted that complaints about police organizational structure were more pronounced in both Female Adult focus group discussions. In this study, female adults were all mothers, and in the majority of cases, were identified as the primary caregiver for their families. Relatedly, they seemed to be the most concerned for their children's safety, as well as the community well-being and welfare of East Athens. This pattern parallels the aforementioned research of Austin and Dodge (1992), Thomas and Holmes (1992), and Campbell et. al (1976), all of whom emphasized higher rates of dissatisfaction among black women. In some contrast to this dissatisfaction with police organizational structure, members of both Female Adult groups agreed that the housing officers deserved some accolades.

But because it's only seven officers, I've got to give them credit too. . . . It's only so much you can do. You got eleven [public housing] developments. Seven for eleven developments. And there are about eight large developments . . . and then you got scattered sites. Well, I mean

please, if you getting so many calls in the large developments and you only got seven officers scattered all over
town . . .

The satisfaction with the housing officers extended to
the new East Athens Initiative sergeant and community officer. As noted in chapter 4, this seemed to result from personal and positive interactions with specific officers and parallels Lasley's et al. (1995) research on the impact of frequent,
personal, and positive citizen-police contacts (see also
Scaglion and Condon, 1980).

However positive, these assessments of individual officers and two of the police units did not temper the Female
Adults' criticism. Nor did they change their perceptions of
being on the receiving end of disparate services, seen as a consequence of this organizational arrangement.

So we don't get quality service. Yet, we pay taxes and we
have to pay the salaries of all the officers. So we don't
want just a public housing officer. We want a police officer. We want a police officer!

LACK OF CITIZEN PARTICIPATION

Citizen support is a necessary component in the coproduction of public services and is an important form of political participation (Brudney and England, 1983; Whitaker,
1980). In this study, lack of citizen participation (i.e., community apathy or passivity) emerged in all focus group discussions. Virtually all participants indicated that they rarely
supported law enforcement efforts either on an individual or
a collective level. This lack of citizen participation supports
Grinc's (1994) emphasis on community apathy or passivity as
an obstacle to community policing. However, some participants did admit to some covert assistance in the form of
nine-one-one calls, calling the "Drug Tip" hot line, and so on.
But generally, as described in chapter 4, residents were afraid

of retribution and reluctant to assist law enforcement in a direct fashion. This fear parallels another finding of Grinc's research on problems in stimulating community involvement and partnerships in community policing (1994), specifically fear of retaliation from drug dealers.

The citizen-focus-group discussions revealed that two community cohorts, which consisted primarily of female participants, were more willing to participate than others. Participants within the Elderly and Female Adult groups expressed a far greater willingness to be supportive of and engage in covert or "behind-the-scene" efforts to improve the general quality of life and well-being of this East Athens community. This finding dramatically contrasts with the statements of participants in the Children and Teenage groups.

These gender and age differences parallel the findings of Ellison and London (1992) who noted that black female adults are significantly more likely than black males and children to join or become active in neighborhood efforts. This also compares to the respective gender as well as age inferences of Chambliss (1994) and Murty et al. (1990). Nonetheless, both Elderly and Female Adult participants were affected and constrained by a genuine fear of retribution.

SUMMARY

This entire focus group research effort speaks to two general conclusions: (1) absolute fear of crime and violence that result from a drug-infested environment and (2) negative perceptions of both police services and community policing. In spite of this unanimity, it is not likely that "group think" occurred in the various focus groups. Rather, in the Nellie B and Vine community, drugs, violence, fear of crime, and negative police-citizen experiences seem to be primary factors. All of this lends support, at least at the perceptual level, to dimensions of the underclass hypothesis of urban service delivery proposed by Lineberry (1977) and supported by Boyle and Jacob (1982) and Bolotin and Cingranelli (1983). The resulting general and negative perceptions of East Athens residents seem to have limited the level of interaction between community residents and community policing officers. This in turn, reinforces the prevailing standards and environment. All of this recalls Austin and Dodge's proposition that

> It is the reality blacks perceive that influences their discontent. They may base their expectations on the past and present of racial inequality and discrimination. (1992:594)

The patterns that emerge contrast to the requirements of community policing, especially the police-community partnership as outlined by Trojanowicz (1982), Trojanowicz and Banas (1985) and Lasley et al. (1995). The lack of citizen involvement is particularly striking since a mutual, coproducing partnership with the community is the cornerstone of the community policing model. However striking, it is clear that it is at least partially the result of perceived disparate service delivery and lack of respect that are themselves fueled by negative interactions with and limited familiarity of police officers (see Fig. 5.1).

Trojanowicz (1982), Trojanowicz and Banas' (1985) and Lasley et al. (1995), all have highlighted the positive effects of foot patrol and bike patrol on African-American communities. These community policing strategies, then, have been found to be an effective tool in altering minority perceptions of, and increasing their satisfaction with, police service delivery. Relatedly, Lasley et al. have concluded that appropriate community policing, police-citizen contacts, in terms of type, frequency, location, and quality, are "an effective tool to 'unfreeze' perceptual gaps between police and citizen . . . even in inner-city neighborhoods" (1995:61).

This is certainly possible in this research site, but it is contingent on more comprehensive implementation of and preparation for community policing. In this, EAI officers must get in touch with the pulse of the community, gain the community's trust, and cultivate community involvement in

a meaningful and effective police-citizen partnership. These
things are possible, even in this community dissatisfied with
police services in general and skeptical about community
policing in particular.

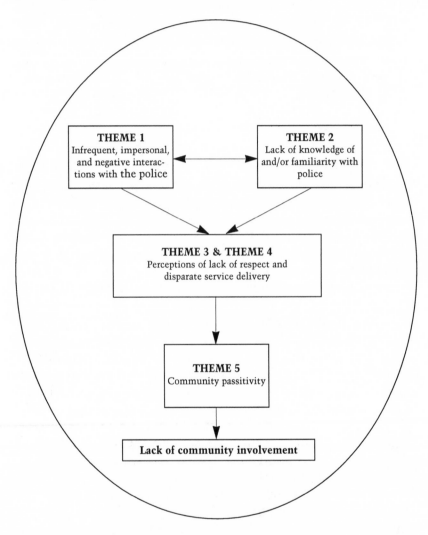

FIGURE 5.1
AN ENVIRONMENT OF FEAR OF CRIME

CHAPTER **6**

POLICY IMPLICATIONS

As noted and analyzed in chapter 5, five themes emerged from focus-group discussions. Related conclusions paralleled some of the empirical findings of previous research on citizen satisfaction with urban service delivery, police service delivery, and the impact of community policing on citizen perceptions and attitudes.

Moreover, this study also shed light on the underpinnings of community apathy and the lack of involvement with police officers. Of particular importance here is the combination of infrequent, impersonal, and negative interactions with police, and lack of knowledge of and familiarity with police officers. This combination in turn seemed to support perceptions of lack of respect and disparate service delivery. When combined with the real and ever present fear of retribution, these inevitably led to passivity and lack of involvement with police and, to some extent, the community. As a result, a general, continual, fear of crime flourishes in this community plagued by drugs and violence.

POLICY IMPLICATIONS

Two major achievements characterized this study. First, this research applied a powerful, yet infrequently used methodology to the study of citizen perspectives on policing in general and community policing in particular. The focus-group methodology used highlighted the perceptions of various cohorts of East Athens residents on police services in general and community policing in particular. Strikingly, this technique yielded a fair amount of consensus, primarily in terms of fear of retribution and negative perceptions of both police services and the community policing effort.

This consensus carries important implications for the design, the expectation(s), the implementation, and the evaluation of community policing efforts.

1. Police departments must commit to the organizational philosophy and strategy of community policing.

Researchers and practitioners have noted the potential misuse of community policing by elected public and police officials, which results in increased politicization of the police function and increased opportunities for police corruption (Carter, 1995; Trojanowicz, Steele & Trojanowicz, 1986). Specifically, community policing has the capacity to be used more as a public relations tool or headline grabber rather than an organizational strategy that promotes a new partnership between the people and their police officers (Bayley, 1988; Klockars, 1988; Manning, 1988; Ross, 1995). On this, Trojanowicz and Bucqueroux warned,

> Improved relations with the community is a welcome by-product of delivering this new form of decentralized and personalized service to the community, rather than its primary goal, as is the case with a public relations effort. (1994:6)

To alleviate this potential problem, elected-public officials and police administrators must be committed to the philosophy and strategy of community policing.

In this present study, East Athens Initiative community policing officers questioned the dedication and commitment of the local police administration and patrolling officers to this organizational strategy or philosophy. Particular concerns focused on the allocation of funds, materials, and other resources. Similarly, EAI officers complained that noncommunity policing officers seemed to diminish their legitimacy and even to question their role as sworn peace officers. Intraorganizational criticism generally took the form of name calling—"love cops," "nigger baby sitters," and "social workers," all of which illustrate the need for departmental commitment. Limited organizational support and lack of peer support, however, are not uncommon (Trojanowicz & Bucqueroux, 1994; Trojanowicz, Steele, & Trojanowicz, 1986; Kratcoski & Noonan, 1995). They have, however, dramatic policy implications, particularly as they relate to the need for departmentwide training and community preparation.

2. Extensive departmentwide "start-up" training is a prerequisite for community policing success and must be adhered to.

    Scholars have noted the importance and significance of "start-up," police departmentwide training, as well as community preparation in laying the cornerstone for this coproduction of police services (Trojanowicz & Bucqueroux, 1994; Brown, 1992; Miller & Hess, 1994; McLaughlin & Donahue, 1995). Yet, lack of adequate "start-up" training for both officers and community residents was evident in this study.

    The inadequacy of training manifested itself in three ways: the lack of interaction and/or lack of personal, positive contact between community policing officers and community residents; lack of knowledge of citizen roles in the community policing undertaking; and the organizational resistance exemplified by noncommunity policing officers. Start-up training is needed, not only with community policing officers and residents within the targeted community, but also with the officers and administrators of the entire police department.

3. Community preparation is a necessity for community involvement and community policing success.

It has been argued that it is the responsibility of the police to promote assertively a partnership between the community and the police (Trojanowicz & Bucqueroux, 1994; Peverly & Phillips, 1993). Citizen police academies (Furguson, 1985; Greenberg, 1991) have been described as an effective and efficient tool, especially as a means

> to open channels of communication, dispel myths and promote understanding between the people and their police, the citizen police academy is increasingly recognized as one of the most important tactics of the public education component of community policing." (Phillips & Peverly, 1993:88)

Systematic training of community residents, then, is needed prior to any community policing initiative.

Some training of residents, combined with departmentwide training of officers, would help to dispel the "blue-suit generalization" phenomenon highlighted in this research. If these training programs occurred, noncommunity policing officers would be aware of the importance of community policing in delivering police services and the potential impact of unnecessarily negative, threatening, impersonal contacts on the perceptions of residents. Citizen contacts with noncommunity policing officers outside the targeted community can have a tremendous effect on citizen attitudes and opinions.

4. Community residents must be targeted and recruited as community policing officers.

Targeting community residents as community policing officers has also emerged as an important policy implication. Direct and personal knowledge of, as well as frequent, positive interaction with a law enforcement officer constituted an important intervening variable in younger residents' perceptions and descriptions of police officers.

Community policing requires, then, recruitment of officers from the targeted area.

This study also suggests that officers should have increased "unofficial" interactions with younger residents to dissipate more formal interactions. For example, the East Athens community policing efforts would benefit from innovative strategies that target younger clients: starting and sponsoring athletic teams; officers volunteering or "hanging out" at the local recreational centers; and/or sponsoring Boy and Girl Scout troops. These efforts would help to tear down the resistance of younger residents, while also developing a positive, nonadversarial relationship between officers and citizens. Officers recruited from the community would be in the best position to do this.

5. Police departments must disseminate realistic time projections on community policing success to temper residents' great expectations.

Community policing success has been properly noted as a long-term phenomenon (Trojanowicz & Bucqueroux, 1994). However, the residents in this study anticipated more "quick fix" solutions. As noted in chapters 4 and 5, Female Adult participants in particular expressed considerable displeasure with the current status of the community policing endeavor, a project that was less than a year old at time of this study. These expectations were clearly unrealistic, especially given the limited nature of the project.

The findings from this research indicate the need for police officers and administrators to project realistic goals and objectives to residents before the implementation of a community policing initiative. These realistic projections should be emphasized in the community preparation phase. This would help to avoid the unrealistic expectations of residents as well as the inevitable dissatisfaction and displeasure with police services and community policing that follow sweeping but unrealistic objectives.

6. Research on the evaluation of community policing and other efforts to coproduce public services must be expanded to include qualitative as well as quantitative methods.

This qualitative, nonexperimental research design proved to be a valuable tool in exploring the perceptions of citizens affected by the East Athens community policing initiative. This study has highlighted the relevance of citizen perceptions in community policing evaluations. These perceptions can be useful in refining community policing ventures, especially as they do not surface in quantitative survey research. This does not suggest that quantitative research should be abandoned. However, it suggests that regular and periodic focus-group interviews can be used in conjunction with survey techniques to keep police departments aware and informed of the perceptions, attitudes, and responses of community residents.

SUMMARY

This research highlights the limitations of the community policing initiative serving the Nellie B and Vine community of East Athens. However, community policing is synonymous with risk-taking and learning by way of trial-and-error.

> Community policing is not "safe." By challenging the status quo and encouraging risk-taking, community policing implicitly includes allowing for failure and embarrassing mistakes. (Trojanowicz & Bucqueroux, 1994:7)

Successful community policing, especially in "alienated" communities, is going to require more than just foot patrols. To ensure the success of this endeavor, a policy champion or entrepreneur who is immune to the rigors of organizational rigidity, "avoidance strategies," and bureaucratic routines is needed (Lipsky, 1980). Additionally, departmental commitment is of paramount importance. This commitment is needed to ensure the increased allocation of program resources and funds, departmentwide training and community preparation, and innovative recruitment strategies. Nonetheless, one must realize that community policing is a long-term phenomenon.

> Community policing is not a quick-fix or panacea. While creative, community-based problem solving can yield immediate successes, community policing also invests in longer-term strategies designed to solve problems and improve the overall quality of life over time. Especially because of its emphasis on positive intervention with juveniles, the full extent of community policing's impact on the community may take years to become fully evident. (Trojanowicz & Bucqueroux, 1994:8)

BIBLIOGRAPHY

Aberbach, Joel, and Jack Walker. "The Attitudes of Blacks Toward City Services: Implications for Public Policy." In *Financing the Metropolis,* ed. John Crecine (Beverly Hills: Sage Publication, 1970).

Adler, L. "To Learn What's on the Consumer's Mind Try Some Focused Group Interviews." *Sales and Marketing Management* 9 (1979): 76–80.

Andersen, Margaret L. "Studying Across Difference: Race, Class, and Gender in Qualitative Research." In John H. Stanfield and Rutledge M. Dennis, eds., *Race and Ethnicity in Research Methods* (Newbury Park, CA: Sage, 1993).

Antunes, George, and John Plumlee. "The Distribution of Urban Public Service." *Urban Affairs Quarterly* 12 (1977): 313–332.

Austin, Roy, and Hiroko Dodge. "Despair, Distrust and Dissatisfaction Among Blacks and Women, 1973–1987," *The Sociological Quarterly* 33:4 (1992) 579–598.

Bachelor, Lynn. "Patterns of Citizen Contacts with a Central Complaint Office: The Case of the Detroit Ombudsman." *State and Local Government Review* 16:2 (Spring 1984): 69–74.

Baer, William C. "Just What Is an Urban Service, Anyway?" *Journal of Politics* 47 (August 1985): 881–898.

Baker, Ralph, and Fred Meyer, Jr. *Evaluating Alternative Law Enforcement Policies* (Lexington, MA.: D.C. Heath and Co., 1979).

Barnett, J. A. "Focusing on Residents." *Journal of Property Management* 54 (1989): 31–32.

Bayley, David H. "Community Policing: A report from the Devils's Advocate." In Jack R. Greene and Stephen D. Mastrofski (eds.) *Community Policing: Rhetoric or Reality?* (New York: Praeger, 1988).

Bayley, David H. "International Differences in Community Policing." In Dennis P. Rosenbaum, ed., *The Challenge of Community Policing: Testing the Promises* (Thousand Oaks, CA: Sage, 1994).

Beale, F. "Double Jeopardy: To Be Black and Female." In *The Black Woman*, ed. by Toni Cade (New York: Signet, 1970).

Beck, Paul, Hal Rainey, and Carol Traut. "Disadvantage, Disaffection, and Race as Divergent Bases for Citizen Fiscal Policy Preferences." *Journal of Politics* 52:1 (Feb. 1990): 71–93.

Bennett, James, and Manuel Johnson. *Better Government at Half the Price: Private Production of Public Services* (Ottawa, IL: Caroline House Publishers, 1981).

Bish, Frances P., and Nancy M. Neubert. "Citizen Contributions to the Productions of Community Safety and Security." In Mark S. Rosentraub, ed., *Financing Local Government: New Approaches to Old Problems* (Ft. Collins, CO: Western Social Science Assoc., 1977).

Bish, Robert, and Vincent Ostrom. *Understanding Urban Government* (Washington, D.C.: American Enterprise Institute, 1973).

Bloch, Peter B. *Equality of Distribution of Police Services: A Case Study of Washington, D.C.* (Washington, D.C.: Urban Institute, 1974).

Boden, W. C. "Flexible Benefits: One Company's View." *Compensation and Benefits Review* 21 (1989): 11–16.

Bolotin, Frederic N. "Distribution of Cutbacks in Local Government Services: A Conceptual Framework." *State and Local Government Review* 22:3 (Fall 1990): 117–122.

Bolotin, Frederic N., and David L. Cingranelli. "Equity and Urban Policy: The Underclass Hypothesis Revisited." *Journal of Politics* 45:1 (Feb. 1983): 209–219.

Bordua, David, and Larry Tifft. "Citizen Interviews, Organizational Feedback, and Police-Community Relations Decisions." *Law and Society Review* 6 (Nov. 1971): 155–182.

Boydstun, John. *San Diego Field Interrogation: Final Report* (Washington D.C.: The Police Foundation, 1975).

Boyle, John, and David Jacobs. "The Intracity Distribution of Services: A Multivariate Analysis." *The American Political Science Review* 76:2 (June 1982): 371–379.

Brandl, Steven, James Frank, Robert Worden, and Timothy Bynum. "Global and Specific Attitudes Toward the Police: Distangling the Relationship." *Justice Quarterly* 11:1 (March 1994): 119–133.

Brown, Karin, and Phillip Coulter. "Subjective and Objective Measures of Police Service Delivery." *Public Administration Review* 43 (1983): 50–58.

Brown, Lee. *Community Policing: A Practical Guide for Police Officers* (Washington, D.C.: National Institute of Justice and Harvard University, Perspective on Policing, No. 12.

Brown, Lee. "Policing in the Nineties: Trends, Issues, and Concerns: Responding to a Changing Environment." *The Police Chief* 58:3 (March 1991): 20–23.

Brown, Lee. "Violent Crime and Community Involvement." *The FBI Law Enforcement Bulletin* 61:5 (May 1992): 2–5.

Brown, S. D. "The Explanation of Particularized Contacting: A Comparison of Models." *Urban Affairs Quarterly* 18 (December 1982): 217–234.

Browning, R., D. Marshall, and D. Tabb. *Protest Is Not Enough* (Berkeley: University of California Press, 1984).

Brudney, Jeffrey. "Coproduction and Local Government—Exploring Other Options for Privatization." *Public Management* (December 1986): 11–13.

Brudney, Jeffrey L. "Evaluating Co-Production Programs." Paper presented at the Annual Meeting of the American Political Science Association, Denver, CO., September 2–5, 1982.

Brudney, Jeffrey, and Robert E. England. "Toward a Definition of the Coproduction Concept." *Public Administration Review* (Jan.–Feb. 1983): 59–65.

Burnett, A., K. Cole, and G. Moon. "Political Participation and Resource Allocation," in *Developments in Political Geography*, ed., M. A. Busteed (London: Academic Press, 1983).

Byars, Peggy, and James Wilcox. "Focus Groups: A Qualitative Opportunity for Researchers." *Journal of Business Communication* 28:1 (Winter 1991): 63–77.

Calder, Bobby Jo. "Focus Groups and the Nature of Qualitative Marketing Research." *Journal of Marketing Research* 14 (1977): 353–364.

Campbell, A. *The Sense of Well-Being in America* (New York: McGraw-Hill, 1981).

Campbell, Alan. "Private Delivery of Public Services." *Public Management* (December 1986): 3–5.

Campbell, Angus, and Howard Schuman. *Racial Attitudes in Fifteen American Cities: Report for the National Advisory Commission on Civil Disorders* (Ann Arbor, MI: Institute for Social Research, 1968).

Campbell, Angus, Phillip E. Converse, and Willard Rodgers. *The Quality of American Life: Perceptions, Evaluations, and Satisfaction* (New York: Russell Sage Foundation, 1976).

Campbell, D. T., and D. W. Fiske. "Convergent and Discriminant Validation by the Multitrait—Multimethod Matrix." *Psychological Bulletin* 56:2 (1959): 81–105.

Capowich, George E., and Jan A. Roehl. "Problem-Oriented Policing: Actions and Effects in San Diego." In Dennis P. Rosenbaum, ed., *The Challenge of Community Policing: Testing the Promises* (Thousand Oaks, CA: Sage, 1994).

Capowich, George E. "Analyzing an Unsuccessful Implementation of Community Policing: An Organizational Case Study." Paper presented at the 1995 Annual Meeting of the Academy of Criminal Justice Sciences, Boston, MA, March 8–11, 1995.

Carter, David L. "Hispanic Interaction with the Criminal Justice System in Texas: Experiences, Attitudes and Perceptions." *Journal of Criminal Justice* 11:3 (1983): 213–227.

Carter, David L. "Community Policing and Political Posturing: Playing the Game." Paper presented at the 1995 Annual Meeting of the Academy of Criminal Justice Sciences, Boston, MA, March 8–11, 1995.

Cashmore, Ellis, and Eugene McLaughlin, eds. *Out of Order: Policing Black People* (New York: Routledge Publishing, 1991).

Chambliss, William. "Policing the Ghetto Underclass: The Politics of Law and Law Enforcement." *Social Problems* 41:2 (May 1994): 177–195.

Christenson, James, and Gregory Taylor. "The Socially Constructed and Situational Context for Assessment of Public Services." *Social Science Quarterly* 64 (1983): 264–274.

Cingranelli, David L. "Race, Politics and Elites: Testing Alternative Models of Municipal Service Distribution." *American Journal of Political Science* 25:4 (Nov. 1981): 664–692.

Cooper, John. *The Police and the Ghetto* (Port Washington, NY: National University Publications, Kennikat Press, 1980).

Cordner, Gary, and Michael Jones. "The Effects of Supplementary Foot Patron on Fear of Crime and Attitudes Toward the Police." In *Issues in Community Policing* eds., Peter Kratcoski and Duane Dukes (Cincinnati: Anderson Publishing Co., 1995).

Coulter, Philip. *Political Voice* (Tuscaloosa, AL: University of Alabama Press, 1988).

Cox, John. "Small Departments and Community Policing." *The FBI Law Enforcement Bulletin* 61:12 (December 1992): 1–6.

Cox, K., J. Higgonbotham, and J. Burton. "Applications of Focus Group Interviews in Marketing." *Journal of Marketing* 40:1 (1976): 77–80.

Cox, Steven, and Jack Fitzgerald. *Police in Community Relations* (Dubuque, IA: Wm. C. Brown Publishers, 1992).

D'Amico-Samuels, Deborah. *Access to Adult Basic Education: African-American Perspectives on Program Guidelines for Recruitment and Retention* (Albany: New York State Department of Education, 1990).

Decker, Scott. "Citizen Attitudes Toward the Police: A Review of Past Findings and Suggestions for Future Policy." *Journal of Police Science and Administration* 9:1 (1981): 81–83.

Decker, Scott, Russell Smith, and Thomas Ulhman. "Does Anything Work? An Evaluation of Urban Police Innovations." In *Evaluating Alternative Law-Enforcement Policies*, eds, Ralph Baker and Fred Meyer, Jr. (Lexington MA: D.C. Heath and Co., 1979): 43–54.

DeHoog, Ruth, David Lowery, and William Lyons. "Citizen Satisfaction with Local Governance: A Test of Individual, Jurisdictional, and City-Specific Explanations." *Journal of Politics* 52:3 (August 1990): 807–837.

Dran, Ellen, and Russell Smith. "Citizen-Initiated Contacting: One More Look." Paper presented at the Annual Meeting of the Midwest Political Science Association, Chicago, April 12.

Durand, Roger. "Some Dynamics of Urban Service Evaluations Among Blacks and Whites." *Social Science Quarterly* 56 (March 1976): 698–706.

Easton, D. *A Framework for Political Analysis* (Englewood Cliffs, NJ: Prentice-Hall, 1965).

Eisinger, Peter. "The Pattern of Citizen Contacts with urban Officials." In Harlan Hahn, ed., *People and Politics in Urban Society* (Beverly Hills, CA: Sage, 1972).

Ellison, Christopher, and Bruce London. "The Social and Political Participation of Black Americans: Compensatory and Ethnic Community Perspectives Revisited." *Social Forces* 70:3 (March 1992): 681–701.

Fay, Brian. *Social Theory and Political Practice* (London: George Allen & Unwin Publishers, 1984).

Fitzgerald, Michael R., and Robert F. Durant. "Citizen Evaluations and Urban Management: Service Delivery in an Era of Protest." *Public Administration Review* 40:6 (Nov./Dec. 1980): 585–594.

Fogelson, Robert. "From Resentment to Confrontation: The Police, The Negroes, and the Outbreak of the Nineteen-Sixties Riots." *Political Science Quarterly* 83:2 (1968): 217–247.

Friedmann, Robert. *Community Policing: Comparative Perspectives and Prospects* (New York: St. Martin's Press, 1992).

Frustenberg, Frank, and Charles Wellford. "Calling the Police: The Evaluation of Police Service." *Law and Society Review* 7 (Spring 1973): 393–406.

Fulwood, Isaac. "Community Empowerment Policing." *The Police Chief* 57:5 (May 1990): 49–51.

Furguson, R. E. "The Citizen Police Academy." *FBI Law Enforcement Bulletin* 54:9 (September 1985): 5–7.

Gamson, William. *Talking Politics* (New York: Cambridge University Press, 1992).

Goldstein, Herman. "Toward Community-Oriented Policing: Potential, Basic Requirements, and Threshold Questions." *Crime and Delinquency* 33 (1987): 29–38.

Goldstein, Herman. *Problem-Oriented Policing* (New York: McGraw Hill, 1990).

Goldwin, Kenneth. "Equal Access versus Selective Access: A Critique of Public Goals Theory." *Public Choice* 29 (Spring 1977) 55.

Greenberg, M. A. "Citizen Police Academies." *FBI Law Enforcement Bulletin*, 60:8, (August 1991):10–13.

Greene, Jack and Ralph Taylor. "Community Based Policing and Foot Patrol: Issues of Theory and Evaluation." In Jack R. Greene and Stephen Mastrofski, eds., *Community Policing: Rhetoric or Reality* (New York: Praeger, 1988).

Greene, Jack R., and Stephen D. Mastrofski. *Community Policing: Rhetoric or Reality* (New York: Praeger, 1988).

Greene, Jack R., William T. Bergman, and Edward J. McLaughlin. "Implementing Community Policing: Cultural and Structural Change in Police Organizations." In Dennis P. Rosenbaum, ed., *The Challenge of Community Policing: Testing the Promises* (Thousand Oaks, CA: Sage, 1994).

Grinc, Randolph M. "'Angels in Marble:' Problems in Stimulating Community Involvement in Community Policing." *Crime and Delinquency* 40:3 (July 1994): 437–468.

Guba, Egen, and Yvonna Lincoln. *Effective Evaluation: Improving the Usefulness of Evaluation Results Through Responsive and Naturalistic Approaches* (San Francisco: Jossey-Bass Publishers, 1981).

Haeberle, Steven. "Good Neighbors and Good Neighborhoods: Comparing Demographic and Environmental Influences on Neighborhood Activism." *State and Local Government Review* 18 (Fall 1986): 109–116.

Hahn, Harlan. "Ghetto Assessments of Police Protection and Authority." *Law and Society Review* 6 (November 1971): 183–194.

Hahn, Harlan. *Police in Urban Society* (Beverly Hills, CA: Sage Publications, 1971).

Hamilton, D., and T. Rose. "Illusory Correlations and the Maintenance of Stereotypic Beliefs." *Journal of Personality and Social Psychology* 39 (1980): 832–845.

Hatry, Harry. *How Effective Are Your Community Services?* (Washington, D.C.: The Urban Institute and ICMA, 1977).

Harwood, Richard. *Citizens and Politics: A View from Main Street America* (Dayton, OH: Kettering Foundation, 1991).

Hawkins v. Town of Shaw. 437 F.2d 1286, 1287 (5th Cir. 1971).

Hero, Rodney. "The Urban Service Delivery Literature: Some Questions and Consideration." *Polity* 18:4 (Summer 1986): 659–677.

Hirschman, Albert. *Exit, Voice and Loyalty* (Cambridge, MA: Harvard University Press, 1970).

Ide, William. "Rebuilding the Public's Trust." *ABA Journal* 79 (September 1993): 8–9.

Inniss, Leslie, and Joe R. Feagin. "The Black 'Underclass' Ideology in Race Relations Analysis." *Social Justice* 16:4 (1989) 13–34.

Jacob, Herbert. "Black and White Perceptions of Justice in the City." *Law and Society Review* 6 (Aug. 1971): 646–668.

Jacob, Herbert. "Contact with Governmental Agencies: A Preliminary Analysis of the Distribution of Government Services." *Midwest Journal of Political Science* 16 (February 1972): 123–146.

Janis, Irving. "The Problem of Validating Content Analysis." In Harold Lasswell et al. (eds.), *Language of Politics* (Cambridge: MIT Press, 1965).

Jarrett, Robin. "Interviewing with Low Income Minority Populations." In David Morgan, ed., *Successful Focus Groups: Advancing the State of the Art* (Newbury Park, CA: Sage, 1993).

Jefferson, Tony. "Discrimination, Disadvantage, and Police-Work." In Ellis Cashmore and Eugene McLaughlin, eds., *Out of Order: Policing Black People* (New York: Routledge, 1991).

Jenkins, Morris. "Fear of the 'Gangsta': African-American Males and the Criminal Justice System." Unpublished paper presented at the Annual Meeting of the Academy of Criminal Justice Sciences, Boston, March 7–11, 1995.

Jones, Bryan D. "Assessing the Products of Government." In *Analyzing Urban-Service Distributions* ed., Richard C. Rich (Lexington: MA: Lexington Books, 1982).

Jones, Bryan, and Clifford Kaufman. "The Distribution of Urban Public Services: A Preliminary Model." *Administration and Society* 6 (November 1974): 337–360.

Jones, Bryan, Saadia Greenberg, and Joseph Drew. *Service Delivery in the City: Citizen Demands and Bureaucratic Rules* (New York: Longman Press, 1980).

Kiser, Larry L., and Stephen L. Percy. "The Concept of Coproduction and Its Implications for Public Service Delivery." Paper Presented at the Annual Meeting of the American Society for Public Administration held in San Francisco, April 13–16, 1980.

Klocars, Carl B. "The Rhetoric of Community Policing." In Jack R. Green and Stephen D. Mastrofski, eds., *Community Policing: Rhetoric or Reality?* New York: Praeger, 1988).

Klocars, Carl B. "Order Maintenance, the Quality of Urban Life, and Police: A Different Line of Argument." In William A. Geller, ed., *Police Leadership in America: Crisis and Opportunity* (New York: Praeger, 1985).

Knodel, John. "The Design and Analysis of Focus Group Studies: A Practical Approach." In David Morgan, ed., *Successful Focus Groups: Advancing the State of the Art* (Newbury Park, CA: Sage, 1993).

Koenig, D. J. "The Effects of Criminal Victimization and Judicial or Police Contacts on Public Attitudes Toward Local Police." *Journal of Criminal Justice* 8 (1980): 243–249.

Kolbert, Elizabeth. "Test-Marketing a President." *The New York Times Magazine*, August 30, 1992, p. 18.

Koven, Steven. "Coproduction of Law Enforcement Services: Benefits and Implications." *Urban Affairs Quarterly* 27:3 (March 1992): 457–470.

Kratcoski, Peter, and Duane Dukes, eds. *Issues in Community Policing* (Cincinnati: Anderson Publishing Co., 1995).

Kratcoski, Peter, Duane Dukes, and Sandra Gustavson. "An Analysis of Citizens' Responses to Community Policing in a Large

Midwestern City." In Peter Kratcoski and Duane Dukes, eds., *Issues in Community Policing* (Cincinnati: Anderson Publishing Co., 1995).

Krippendorff, Klaus. *Content Analysis: An Introduction To Its Methodology* (Beverly Hills: Sage Publication, 1980).

Krueger, Richard. *Focus Groups: A Practical Guide For Applied Research* (Newbury Park, CA: Sage Publications, 1988).

Lasley, James, and Robert Vernon. "Police-Citizen Partnerships in the Inner City." *FBI Law Enforcement Bulletin* (May 1992):18–22.

Lasley, James, Robert Vernon, and George Dery III. "Operation Cul-de-Sac: LAPD's 'Total Community' Policing Program." In Peter Kratcoski and Duane Dukes, eds., *Issues in Community Policing* (Cincinnati: Anderson Publishing, 1995).

Laswell, Harold. *Politics: Who Gets What, When, and How?* (New York: McGraw Hill, 1938).

Lederman, Linda. "Assessing Educational Effectiveness: The Focus Group Interview as a Technique for Data Collection." *Communication Education* 38 (April 1990): 119–127.

Lederman, Linda. "If You Want To Know What They Think, Ask Them: Using the Focus Group Interview for Communication Research." A paper prepared for and presented at the 79th Annual Eastern Communication Association Conference, Baltimore, MD (April 1988).

Lee, Seung Jong. "Policy Type, Bureaucracy, and Urban Policies: Integrating Models of urban Service Distribution." *Policy Studies Journal* 22:1 (Spring 1994): 87–109.

Lehman, K. L. *A Study of the Anti-Smoking Campaign.* Unpublished doctoral dissertation (1987), Bowling Green State University, Ohio.

Lengua, Lillana, Mark Roosa, Erika Schupak-Neuberg, Marcia Michaels, Carolyn Berg, Louis Weschler. "Using Focus Groups to Guide the Development of a Parenting Program for Difficult-to-Reach, High Risk Families." *Family Relations* 41 (April 1992): 163–168.

Levy, Frank, Arnold Meltsner, and Aaron Wildavsky. *Urban Outcomes* (Berkeley: University of California Press, 1974).

Lineberry, Robert. *Equality and Urban Policy: The Distribution of Municipal Public Services* (Beverly Hills: Sage, 1977).

Lineberry, Robert, and Robert Welch. "Who Gets What: Measuring The Distribution of Urban Public Services." *Social Science Quarterly* 54:4 (March 1974): 700–712.

Lipsky, Michael. *Street-level Bureaucracy* (New York: Russell Sage Foundation, 1980).

Maddox, Joseph. "Community Sensitivity." *The FBI Law Enforcement Bulletin* 62:2 (February 1993): 10–12.

Manning, Peter K. "Community Policing as a Drama of Control. In Jack R. Greene and Stephen D. Mastrofski, eds., *Community Policing: Rhetoric or Reality?* (New York: Praeger, 1988).

Marans, R., and W. Rodgers. "Toward an Understanding of Community Satisfaction." In A.H. Hawley and V.P. Rock, eds., *Metropolitan America in Contemporary Perspective* (Beverly Hills: Sage, 1975).

Martin, L. *Library Response to Urban Change* (Chicago: American Library Association, 1969).

Mastrofski, Stephen D. "Community Policing as Reform: A Cautionary Tale." In Jack R. Greene and Stephen D. Mastrofski, eds., *Community Policing: Rhetoric or Reality* (New York: Praeger, 1988).

McLaughlin, Vance, and Michael Donahue. "Training for Community-Oriented Policing." In Peter Kratcoski and Duane Dukes, eds., *Issues in Community Policing* (Cincinnati: Anderson Publishing Co., 1995).

Merton, Robert, Marjorie Fiske, and Patricia Kendall. *The Focused Group Interview* (Glencoe, IL: Free Press, 1956).

Metchik, Eric, and Ann Winton. "Community Policing and Its Implications for Alternative Models on Police Officer Selection." In Peter Kratcoski and Duane Dukes, eds., *Issues in Community Policing* (Cincinnati: Anderson Publishing Co., 1995).

Milbrath, Lester, and M. L. Goel. *Political Participation* (Skokie, IL: Rand McNally, 1977).

Miller, Linda S., and Karen M. Hess. *Community Policing: Theory and Practice* (Minneapolis/St. Paul: West Publishing Co., 1994).

Miranda, Rowan and Ittipone Tunyavong. "Patterned Inequality? Reexamining the Role of Distributive Politics in Urban Service Delivery." *Urban Affairs Quarterly* 29:4 (June 1994): 509–535.

Mladenka, Kenneth. "The Urban Bureaucracy and the Chicago Political Machine: Who Gets What and the Limits to Political Control." *American Political Science Review* 74 (1980) 991–998.

Mladenka, Kenneth R., and Kim Quaile Hill. "The Distribution of Urban Police Services." *The Journal of Politics* 40:1 (February 1978): 112–133.

Moore, Mark. "Problem Solving and Community Policing." In *Modern Policing*, eds., Michael Tonry and Norwal Morris (Chicago: Univ. of Chicago Press, 1992).

Moore, Mark, and Darrel Stephens. *Beyond Command and Control: The Strategic Management of Police Departments* (Washington D.C.: Police Executive Research Forum, 1991).

Morgan, David. *Focus Groups as Qualitative Research* (Newbury Park, CA: Sage Publications, 1988).

Murty, Komanduri, Julian Roebuck, and Joann Smith. "The Image of the Police in Black Atlanta Communities." *Journal of Police Science and Administration* 17:4 (1990): 250–257.

Nardulli, Peter, and Jeffrey Stonecash. *Politics, Professionalism, and Urban Services, the Police* (Cambridge, MA: Oelgeschlager, Gun and Hain, 1981).

Norris, Clive, Nigel Fielding, Charles Kemp, and Jane Fielding. "Black and Blue: An Analysis of the Influence of Race on Being Stopped by The Police." *The British Journal of Sociology* 43:2 (1992): 207–225.

O'Brien, John. "Public Attitudes Toward the Police." *Journal of Police Science and Administration* 6:3 (Sept. 1978): 299–314.

O'Donnell, J. M. "Focus Groups: A Habit Forming Evaluation Technique." *Training and Development Journal* 42 (1988): 71–73.

Ostrom, Elinor, ed. *The Delivery of Urban Services: Outcomes of Change* (Beverly, Hills, CA: Sage, 1975).

Ostrom, Vincent, and Frances Bish. *Comparing Urban Service Delivery Systems* (Beverly Hills, CA: Sage Publications, 1977).

Ostrom, Vincent, and Elinor Ostrom. "Public Goods Versus Public Choices." In E.S. Savas, ed., *Alternatives for Delivering Public Services—Toward Improved Performance* (Boulder, CO: Westview Press, 1977).

Parks, Roger. "Police Responses to Victimization: Effects on Citizen Attitudes and Perception." In Wesley Skogan, ed. *Sample Survey of the Victims of Crime* (Cambridge MA: Ballinger, 1976): 89–104.

Parks, Roger. "Linking Objective and Subjective Measures of Performance." *Public Administration Review* 44 (1984): 118–127.

Pate, Tony, Amy Ferrara, Robert Bowers, and Jon Lorence. *Police Response Time: Its Determinants and Effects* (Kansas City, MO: Midwest Research Institute, Police Foundation, 1976).

Patton, Michael Quinn. *Qualitative Evaluation and Research Methods* (Newbury Park, CA: Sage, 1990).

Pennell, Frances. "Private versus Collective Strategies for Dealing with Crime, Citizen Attitudes Toward Crime, and the Police in Urban Neighborhoods." *Journal of Voluntary Action Research* 7:1–2 (1978): 59–74.

Pepinsky, Harold. "Issues of Citizen Involvement in Policing." *Crime and Delinquency* 35:3 (July 1989): 458–470.

Percy, Stephen L. "Citizen Coproduction of Community Safety." In Ralph Baker and Fred A. Meyer, Jr., eds., *Evaluating Alternative Law Enforcement Policies* (Lexington, MA: Lexington Books, 1979).

Percy, Stephen L. "Conceptualizing and Measuring Citizen Coproduction of Community Safety." *Policy Studies Journal* 7 (1978): 486–493.

Percy, Stephen L., Larry L. Kiser, and Roger Parks. "Citizen Coproduction: A Neglected Dimension of Public Service Delivery." Working Paper W80–31. (Bloomington Indiana: Indiana University, Workshop in Political Theory and Policy Analysis, 1980.)

Peverly, William, and Peter Phillips. "Community Policing Through Citizen Police Academies." *The Police Chief* 60:8 (August 1993): 89–91.

Poister, Theodore, and James McDavid. "Citizen Evaluations of Police Performance: Police-Citizen Interactions in the Context of Criminal Victimization." Paper presented at the Annual Conference of the American Society for Public Administration, Washington D.C. (1976).

Radelet, Louis. *The Police and the Community*, 4th ed. (New York: Macmillan, 1986).

Radelet, Louis, and David Carter. *The Police and the Community*, 5th ed. (New York: Macmillan Publishing Co., 1994).

Rehfuss, John. Contracting Out in Government: A Guide to Working with Outside Contractors to Supply Public Service (San Francisco: Jossey-Bass Publishers, 1989).

Report of the National Advisory Commission on Civil Disorders (Washington, D.C.: U.S. Government Printing Office, 1968).

Rich, Richard, ed. *Analyzing Urban-Service Distributions* (Lexington, MA: Lexington Books, 1982).

Rich, Richard, ed. *The Politics of Urban Public Services* (Lexington, MA: Lexington Books, 1982).

Rich, Richard. "The Roles of Neighborhood Organizations in Urban Service Delivery." *Urban Affairs Papers* 1 (Fall, 1979): 81–93

Rich, Richard. "Voluntary Action and Public Services." *Journal of Voluntary Action Research* 7:1–2 (1978): 4–14.

Rosenbaum, Dennis, P. *Community Policing: Testing the Promises* (Thousand Oaks, CA: Sage, 1994).

Rosentraub, Mark S., and Karen S. Harlow. "The Coproduction of Police Services: A Case Study of Citizens' Inputs in the Production of Personal Safety." Paper presented at the Annual Meetings of the American Society for Public Administration held in San Francisco, April 13–16, 1980.

Rosentraub, Mark S., and Elaine Sharp. "Consumers as Producers of Social Services: Coproduction and the Level of Social Services." *Southern Review of Public Administration* (1981).

Ross, Jeffrey Ian. "Confronting Community Policing: Minimizing Community Policing as Public Relations." In Peter C. Kratcoski and Duane Dukes, eds., *Issues in Community Policing* (Cincinnati: Anderson Publishing, 1995).

Rossi, Peter H., Richard A. Beck, and Bettye K. Eidson. *The Roots of Urban Discontent* (New York: John Wiley & Sons, 1974).

Rossi, Peter H., and Eugene Groves. "Police Perceptions of a Hostile Ghetto: Realism or Projection." *American Behavioral Scientist* 13 (May-August 1970): 727–743.

Ruchelman, Leonard. *A Workbook in Redesigning Public Services* (Albany: State University of New York Press, 1989).

Rundquist, B., and J. Ferejohn. "Observation on a Distributive Theory of Policy Making." In C. Liske, W. Loehr, and J. McCamant, eds., *Comparative Public Policy* (New York: Wiley Publishing, 1975).

Saint-Germain, Michelle, Tamsen Bassford, and Gail Montano. "Surveys and Focus Groups in Health Research with Older Hispanic Women." *Qualitative Health Research* 3:3 (August 1993): 341–367.

Savas, E. S. *Alternatives for Delivering Public Services Toward Improved Performance* (Boulder, CO: Westview Press, 1977).

Savas, E. S. "Alternative Structural Models for Delivering Urban Services." In Arthur Swersey and Edward Ignall, eds., *Studies in the Management Sciences: Delivery of Urban Services* (New York: North-Holland, 1986).

Scaglion, Richard, and Richard Condon. "Determinants of Attitude Toward City Police." *Criminology* 17:4 (1980): 485–494.

Schumaker, Paul, and Russell Getter. "Structural Sources of Unequal Responsiveness to Group Demands in American Cities." *Western Political Quarterly* 36 (March 1983): 7–29.

Schuman, Howard, and Barry Gruenberg. "Dissatisfaction with City Services: Is Race an Important Factor?" In Harlan Hahn, ed., *People and Politics in Urban Society* (Beverly Hills: Sage, 1972).

Seader, David. "Privatization and America's Cities." *Public Management* (December 1986): 6–9.

Sears, David, and Jack Citrin. *Tax Revolt* (Cambridge: Harvard University Press, 1982).

Seidel, J. V., and J. A. Clark. "The Ethnograph: A Computer Program for the Analysis of Qualitative Data." *Qualitative Sociology* 7 (1984): 110–125.

Sharp, Elaine. "Citizen-Initiated Contacting of Government Officials and Socioeconomic Status: Determining the Relationship and Accounting for It." *American Political Science Review* 76 (1982): 109–115.

Sharp, Elaine. *Citizen Organizations and Participation in Law Enforcement Advocacy and Coproducton: The Role of Incentives.* Ph.D. Dissertation. (Chapel Hill, NC: University of North Carolina at Chapel Hill, Department of Political Science, 1978.)

Sharp, Elaine. "Citizen Organizations in Policing Issues and Crime Prevention: Incentives for Participation." *Journal of Voluntary Action Research* 7:1–2 (1978): 45–58.

Sharp, Elaine. "Toward a New Understanding of Urban Services and Citizen Participation: The Coproduction Concept." *Midwest Review of Public Administration* 14:2 (June 1980): 105–118.

Sharp, Elaine B. *Urban Politics and Administration* (White Plains, New York: Longman, 1990).

Shin, Doh, and David Everson. "Participation in Verba-Nie Models in Three Middle-Sized Cities." Paper presented at the annual meeting of the Midwest Political Science Association, Chicago, April 23–26, 1980.

Sill, Patricia L. "Community-Oriented Policing and Crime Prevention Training: A Must for the Nineties." *The Police Chief* 58:11 (November 1991): 56–58.

Skogan, Welsley G. "Citizen Satisfaction with Police Services." In *Evaluating Alternative Law-Enforcement Policies*, eds. Ralph Baker and Fred A. Meyer, Jr. (Lexington, Mass.: D.C. Heath and Co, 1979): 29–42.

Skogan, Wesley. *Disorder and Decline: Crime and the Spiral Decay in American Neighborhoods* (Berkeley: University of California Press, 1990).

Skolnick, Jerome and David Bayley. *The New Blue Line: Police Innovations in Six American Cities* (New York: Free Press, 1986).

Sloan, Ron, Robert Trojanowicz, and Bonnie Bucqueroux. *Basic Issues in Training: A Foundation for Community Policing* (East Lansing, MI: National Center for Community Policing Publishing, Michigan State University.

Sower, Christopher. *Community Involvement* (Glencoe, IL.: Free Press, 1957).

Sparrow, Malcolm, Mark Moore, and David Kennedy. *Beyond 911* (New York: Basic Books, 1990).

Stanfield, John H. "Methodological Reflections: An Introduction." In John H. Stanfield and Rutledge M. Dennis, eds., *Race and Ethnicity In Research Methods* (Newbury Park, CA: Sage, 1993).

Stanfield, John H. "Epistemological Considerations." In John H. Stanfield and Rutledge M. Dennis, eds., *Race and Ethnicity In Research Methods* (Newbury Park, CA: Sage, 1993).

Stanfield, John H., and Rutledge M. Dennis, eds. *Race and Ethnicity In Research Methods* (Newbury Park, CA: Sage, 1993).

Stewart, David, and Prem Shamdasani. *Focus Groups: Theory and Practice* (Newbury Park, CA: Sage Publications, 1990).

Stewart, James. "The Urban Strangler: How Crime Causes Poverty in the Inner City." *Policy Review* 37 (Jan. 1986): 2–6.

Stipak, Brian. *Citizens' Evaluation of Municipal Services in Los Angeles County* (Los Angeles: Institute of Government and Public Affairs, University of California, 1974).

Stone, Clarence. *Regime Politics: Governing Atlanta 1947–1980* (Lawrence, KS: University Press of Kansas, 1989).

Swanstrom, Todd. *The Crisis of Growth Politics; Cleveland, Kucinich, and the Challenge of Urban Populism* (Philadelphia: Temple University Press, 1985).

Syzbillo, George, and Robert Berger. "What Advertising Agencies Think of Focus Groups." *Journal of Advertising Research* 19:3 (1979): 29–33.

Templeton, Jane. *Focus Groups: A Guide for Marketing and Advertising Professionals* (Chicago: Probus, 1987).

Thomas, John. "Citizen-Initiated Contacts with Government Agencies: A Test of Three Theories." *American Journal of Political Science* 26 (August 1982): 504–522.

Thomas, Melvin E., and Bernadette Holmes. "Determinants of Satisfaction for Blacks and Women. *The Sociological Quarterly* 33:3 (1992): 459–472.

Toulmin, Llewellyn. "Equity as a Decision Rule in Determining the Distribution of Urban Public Services." *Urban Affairs Quarterly* 23:3 (1988): 389–413.

Trojanowicz, Robert. *An Evaluation of the Neighborhood Foot Patrol Program in Flint, Michigan* (East Lansing, MI: National Center for Community Policing, Michigan State University, 1982).

Trojanowicz, Robert. "Building Support for Community Policing." *The FBI Law Enforcement Bulletin* 61:5 (May 1992): 7–13.

Trojanowicz, Robert, and Dennis Banas. *The Impact of Foot Patrol on Black and White Perceptions of Policing* (East Lansing, MI:

National Neighborhood Foot Patrol Center, Michigan State University, School of Criminal Justice, 1985).

Trojanowicz, Robert, and Dennis Banas. *Perceptions of Safety: A Comparison of Foot Patrol Versus Motor Patrol Officers* (East Lansing, MI: National Neighborhood Foot Patrol Center, Michigan State University, School of Criminal Justice, 1985).

Trojanowicz, Robert, and David Carter. "The Changing Face of America." *The FBI Law Enforcement Bulletin* 59:1 (January 1990): 6–12.

Trojanowicz, Robert, and Bonnie Bucqueroux. "The Community Policing Challenge." *Police Technology and Management* 1:4 (November 1990): 40–44, 51.

Trojanowicz, Robert, and Bonnie Bucqueroux. *Community Policing: A Contemporary Perspective* (Cincinnati: Anderson Publishing, 1990).

Trojanowicz, Robert, and Bonnie Bucqueroux. *Community Policing: How to Get Started* (Cincinnati: Anderson Publishing, 1994).

Trojanowicz, Robert, and Mark H. Moore. *The Meaning of Community Policing* (East Lansing, MI: National Neighborhood Foot Patrol Center, Michigan State University, School of Criminal Justice, 1988).

Trojanowicz, Robert, Marilyn Steele, and Susan Trojanowicz. *Community Policing: A Taxpayer's Perspective* (East Lansing, MI: National Neighborhood Foot Patrol Center, School of Criminal Justice, Michigan State University).

Trojanowicz, Susan. "Theory of Community Policing." Unpublished Thesis for Masters of Science Degree. Michigan State University, East Lansing, Michigan (1992).

Tumin, Zachary. "Managing Relations with the Community." Working Paper no. 86-05-06. Cambridge, MA: Harvard University, JFK School of Government (1986).

Valente, C. F., and L. D. Manchester. "Rethinking Local Services: Examining Alternative Delivery Approaches." *ICMA Special Report* 12 (March 1984): i–xii.

Vedlitz, Arnold, James Dyer, and Roger Durand. "Citizen Contacts with Local Government: A Comparative View." *American Journal of Political Science* 24 (February 1980): 50–67.

Verba, Sydney, and Norman Nie. *Participation In America: Political Democracy and Social Equality* (New York: Harper and Row, 1972).

Viteritti, Joseph. *Police, Politics, and Pluralism in New York City: A Comparative Case Study* (Beverly Hills, CA: Sage, 1973).

Walker, Christopher R., and Sandra-Gail Walker. "The Citizen and the Police: A Partnership in Crime Prevention." *Canadian Journal of Criminology* 32:1 (January 1990): 125–135.

Walker, Darlene, Richard Richardson Oliver Williams, Thomas Deyner, and Skip McGaughey. "Contact and Support: An Empirical Assessment of Public Attitudes Toward the Police and the Courts." *North Carolina Law Review* 51 (Nov. 1972): 43–79.

Weatheritt, Mollie. "Community Policing: Does It Work and How Do We Know?" In T. Bennett, ed., *The Future of Policing* (Cambridge, UK: Institute of Criminology, 1983).

Weatheritt, Mollie. "Community Policing Now." In P. Willmott, ed., *Policing and The Community* (London, UK: Policy Studies Institute, 1987).

Webe, Robert. *Basic Content Analysis* (Beverly Hills: Sage Publications, 1980).

Weicher, J. C. "The Allocation of Police Protection by Income Class." *Urban Studies* 8 (1971) 207–220.

Whitaker, Gordon. "Coproduction: Citizen Participation in Service Delivery." *Public Administration Review* 40:3 (May/June 1980): 240–246.

White, Melvin, and Ben Menke. "A Critical Analysis of Survey on Public Opinion Toward Police Agencies." *Journal of Police Science and Administration* 6:2 (Aug. 1978): 204–218.

Wilbern, Y., and L. A. Williams. "City Taxes and Services: Citizens Speak Out." *Nation's Cities* 9 (August 1971): 9–24.

Wilcox, James. *Professional Focus Group Moderator* (Bowling Green, OH: Bowling Green State University, 1988).

Williams, Oliver. "Life-Style Values and Political Decentralization in Metropolitan Areas." In *Urban Politics: Past, Present and Future*, eds. H. Hahn and C. Levine (New York: Longman, 1980): 207–223.

Williams, Thomas. *Citizen's Evaluations of Local Government Service in a Southern Community: Determinants of Support* (Washington, D.C.: National Association of Schools of Public Affairs and Administration, 1977).

Wilson, James Q. *Bureaucracy* (New York: Basic Books, 1989).

Wilson, James, and George Kelling. "Broken Windows: The Police and Neighborhood Safety." *Atlantic Monthly* (March 1992): 29–38.

Wolch, Jennifer. "Spatial Consequences of Social Policy: The Role of Service-Facility Location in Urban Development Patterns." In Richard Rich, ed., *The Politics of Urban Public Services* (Lexington, MA: Lexington Books, 1982).

Wycoff, Mary Ann, and Wesley G. Skogan. "Community Policing in Madison: An Analysis of Implementation and Impact." In Dennis P. Rosenbaum, ed., *The Challenge of Community Policing: Testing the Promises* (Thousand Oaks, CA: Sage, 1994).

Yates, Douglas. *The Ungovernable City: The Politics of Urban Policymaking* (Cambridge, MA: The MIT Press, 1977).

INDEX